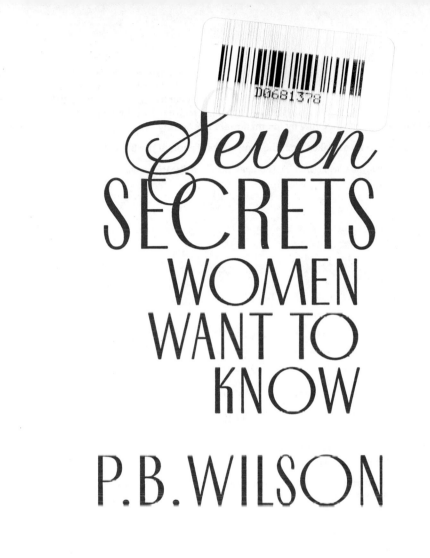

Seven SECRETS WOMEN WANT TO KNOW

P.B. WILSON

HARVEST HOUSE PUBLISHERS
Eugene, Oregon 97402

Cover design by Koechel Peterson & Associates, Minneapolis, Minnesota

SEVEN SECRETS WOMEN WANT TO KNOW
Copyright © 2000 by P.B. Wilson
Published by Harvest House Publishers
Eugene, Oregon 97402

Library of Congress Cataloging-in-Publication Data
Wilson, P.B. (P. Bunny), 1950–
    Seven secrets women want to know / P.B. Wilson
        p. cm.
    ISBN 0-7369-0165-5
        1. Christian women—Religious life. I. Title: Seven secrets women want to
    know. II. Title.
    BV4527.W557 2000
    248.8'43—dc21

                                                                00-028128

Printed in the United States of America.

00 01 02 03 04 05 06 07 / BC-BG / 10 9 8 7 6 5 4 3 2

*To Dorice, Christine, Mealoofa, Angela, Ta'atele, and Bettina.
Thank you for blessing my life with
your devoted service.*

Acknowledgments

There are certain friends who avail themselves to me while I'm writing my books. They read and reread my material, while asking questions, making comments, and looking for typos. I would like to especially thank Mary Dumas for the countless hours spent reviewing this book. I so appreciate your dedication and friendship.

To Susie Kimes, an incredible woman of God who "provokes me to love and good works" just by her presence. Your help on this project was invaluable. And to Sandi Snavely. I feel like waiting at the mailbox for your response to what I have written. You are so encouraging and honest and it's like a breath of fresh air.

I would also like to thank Marilyn Beaubien, Marilyn Davis, Barbara Calhoun, Yvette Reynolds, and Yvonne Stewart for your assistance with this project.

And then there is Frank, my husband. The man I reverence and adore. My "bridge over troubled water," my encourager, lover, and best friend. You've helped me through once again. I continue to thank God for loving me so much that He led you to me.

Contents

1

Up, Up, and Away

Lord, I want to soar on eagles' wings…

Removing her special gift from its bag, I heard my seven-year-old daughter, Gabrielle, squeal with excitement. Her new toy had traveled across the country neatly tucked away in my suitcase. Now we were ready to share the fun guaranteed by this amusing object. It came in two parts—a mushroom-shaped base with a pull string, and a colorful stick-like insert attached to a round propeller at the top. The instructions were simple enough: Put the stick in the base and pull the string. The stick, with its animated character holding on, would fly up to 10 feet in the air!

It was a perfect California autumn day. The air was warm and delightfully clear, and our courtyard made an excellent launching pad. Gabrielle could hardly stand still as she waited for me to send the toy into space. Smiling, I pulled the string, and she and I watched. The propeller whirled and whirled but never left its base. After a few more attempts, Gabrielle impatiently took the toy from my hands, convinced she could make it work. She pulled and pulled and the propeller whirled over and over again. But the toy still remained fixed in its original position.

I read the directions carefully to see if we might have overlooked something. However the truth was becoming all too apparent—Gabrielle's toy was simply not functioning properly. Taking a deep breath, I broke the news to my daughter that her gift would need to be returned to the store for a replacement.

At first Gabrielle refused to believe me. "No, Mommy!" she exclaimed. "Please don't take it back. It works just fine!"

While I was shaking my head in disagreement, she announced, "It will be okay, Mom. Look, I'll keep it until the summertime, and on a real hot day it can be my fan!"

With that, she began pulling the string again. As the propeller whirled she pointed it toward her face, demonstrating how her new-toy-gone-bad could be used for an alternative purpose. Impressed by her quick adjustment, I laughed, "No, Gabrielle, that's a good idea, but it wasn't designed to be a fan. It was created to fly."

Later that evening, after tucking her into bed and turning out her light, I thought about how many of us are like that toy. Too often we settle for what appears to be productive, spinning around in the same place when in fact we were created by God to fly. Isaiah 40:31 says, "But those who hope in the LORD will renew their strength. They will soar on wings like eagles…"

The "S" Factor

I spent all of my single years and some of my married life in a no-fly position, and that has kindled a desire in me to invest time in a book to encourage other women. A few months ago, I found myself sitting on a plane with pen and paper, beginning to write down practiced principles that loosed the emotional and mental bondage which had held me imprisoned. To my surprise, the seven words that enabled me to take flight all began with the letter "s."

Since then, I have continued to explore more in-depth those seven secrets, which I have come to affectionately call "The 'S' Factor." Some of these principles are controversial. However, as I will show, most of the controversy is due to misunderstanding and wrong application. Besides, whatever the arguments, the Bible consistently demonstrates the power and freedom that can be found in each precept.

The seven secret principles every woman wants to know are:

- Submission

- Servanthood

- Seasons

- Success

- Sacrificial love

- Suffering (long-suffering)

- Steadfastness

Maybe you're wondering, "What makes these principles secrets?"

The answer is that secrets are whispered, not openly discussed. Submission, servanthood, and long-suffering are the bedrock of our walk with Christ. But when was the last time you heard those subjects talked about in a positive manner among a group of women? I thought so. That makes them secrets.

According to that guideline, it may seem that the other four principles are not secrets. Seasons, success, sacrificial love, and steadfastness in the study of God's Word are proclaimed from many pulpits. Seminars concerning each point are held in abundance. But they become secrets when they are directly tied to submission, servanthood, and long-suffering. Those three elements change the equation and directly affect how the latter principles work in our lives.

Why do women want to know these secrets? *Because as Christian women, we should want what God wants.* Understanding and practicing these precepts will cause us to reach for, and then live in, the peace God has designed for us. He offers contentment, no matter how chaotic the world around us may be.

Building a Strong Base

Remember Gabrielle's toy that was unable to fly? After checking with the manufacturer, we learned that the toy had a faulty base. Life is like that. God created us to be launched from a spiritual base connected to Him.

> *"...but those who hope in the LORD will renew their strength. They will soar on wings like eagles..."*
> *(Isaiah 40:31).*

Maybe you're like me. Early in my life I knew nothing about the need for a spiritual base. But at the same time I had an itch I couldn't scratch and a void I couldn't fill. Money, men, a successful career, friends, and material possessions didn't fill the void. It was as if an invisible vacuum was sucking out everything I tried to pour into it. I was disconnected from God.

It was during this time that someone asked me the question, "Did you know that Jesus Christ claimed to be God?"

That was a jarring inquiry, and I pondered its implications. Sure, Jesus had claimed to be the *Son* of God. But God Himself? To my knowledge, no prophet or messenger had ever claimed to *be* God (other than those we would deem to be insane). My friend continued, "Either He was a liar, the greatest con man the world has known, or He was who He claimed to be. And Bunny, your eternal life will be determined by the answer."

I began to realize that the conclusions I had reached regarding spiritual matters were drawn from other people's opinions. To me, the Bible was a book that had been written by men who wanted to suppress women. Furthermore, I believed it was full of contradictions. But where had I gotten my information? I'd done no real research myself.

Taking up the challenge, I began to do my own study. After considerable effort, I came to the conclusion that if any book had been written by God, it would have to be the Bible. It took over 1,500 years and over 37 authors to write it. They were from different cultural, geographical, and educational backgrounds, yet they never disagreed with each other. How could that be possible? It wasn't. It's impossible.

If the names of the books of the Bible and the introductions to each chapter were removed, it would be difficult to determine who wrote each book. What makes this so fascinating is that a man like Moses was highly educated while Nehemiah, a cupbearer to a king, was unschooled. The Apostle Paul spoke several languages fluently while John and Peter were uneducated fishermen. Surely we could tell the difference between the writings of a college professor and the work of someone who didn't attend school. Not so in the Bible. It reads as one book. How is that possible? It's impossible.

The Bible is a miracle. In 2 Timothy 3:16, Paul explains its incredible consistency when he says, "All scripture is given by inspiration of God..." (KJV).

Once I finally came to the conclusion that the Bible was written by God, exploring the question of whether Jesus was God became my next pursuit. And it didn't take me long to confirm that He was. His story is clear. His life was prophesied hundreds of years before He arrived. Prophets foretold where He would be born and raised, what He would do during His lifetime, and how He would die. Every "i" had to be dotted and every "t" crossed in order for Him to be the Christ. And every one of those prophecies was fulfilled.

The Jewish leaders knew that Jesus claimed to be God. In John 10:31 we read:

> *Again the Jews picked up stones to stone him, but Jesus said to them, "I have shown you many great miracles from the Father. For which of these do you stone me?" "We were not stoning you for any of these," replied the Jews, "but for blasphemy, because you, a mere man, claim to be God."*

Yes, Jesus did claim to be God. But how does that affect us?

If Jesus is who He says He is, then His statements take on a new meaning. In John 14:6, Jesus declares, "I am the way and the truth and the life. No one comes to the Father except through me." Neither Confucius nor Buddha nor Mohammed can get to the Father unless he goes through Jesus. Why? Because Jesus died on the cross for our sins and rose from the grave so that we might have eternal life. Deciding on who

Jesus is determines our eternal destiny. Once we conclude that He is indeed the Son of God and God the Son, we then must take seriously His teachings about eternal life.

Not Long for This World

Almost everyone remembers the day Princess Diana was killed in an automobile accident. I was at a retreat center, and when it was first reported that she was hurt, I thought about the days or maybe even months it would take for her to recover. Then, before I knew it, the newscaster was saying, "It has been confirmed that Princess Diana is dead." I couldn't believe my ears; it seemed surreal. Like the rest of the world, I was in shock. And as the news sank in, one thing became glaringly clear—it doesn't matter whether you are homeless or an international icon; you are not in control of life or death.

Whether it's the tragedy of Princess Diana or the loss of a friend or loved one, death quickly reminds us that earth is a temporary place. There will come a time when we are called away from here, and as the saying goes, "No one gets out alive."

But maybe it wasn't death that first grabbed your eternal attention. Perhaps you were standing beneath the night sky—a black canopy where it looked as though God had flipped a switch and the stars had responded in full splendor. When I look up at that great expanse, a feeling of insignificance overpowers me. It makes me wonder why God would care about little ol' me so much that He would send His only Son to die on a cross for my sins.

That is why, during our sojourn here on earth, the Bible requires us to make a decision about Jesus Christ and our spiritual condition. In Romans 3:23 Paul writes, "...for all have sinned and fall short of the glory of God...." That means no one qualifies on his or her own merit to have a relationship with God. We must agree with His Word that we are sinners.

The next step is to obey Romans 10:9, which promises, "...if you confess with your mouth, 'Jesus is Lord,' and believe in your heart [the decision making center of your life] that God raised him from the dead, you will be saved [from eternal separation from God]."

Until we come to know Jesus as our Savior through repentance from sin and faith in Him, our base is broken. But when we take the steps to receive Him as Lord, the base is repaired and we are now ready to be positioned for flight. Do we just automatically fly? No, the string has to be pulled first. The spiritual propulsion we need to soar comes from the study and application of God's Word, the Bible.

The task of getting trained and activated by God's Word offers no compromise, no alibi, no justification for not getting the job done. "Be ye doers of the word, and not hearers only" (James 1:22 KJV) becomes our motto. The more we respond to God's instructions, the higher we fly. He literally takes us from glory to glory (see 2 Corinthians 3:18).

Each time we learn a principle or precept, the string is pulled and we go higher and higher. What an exciting adventure to be in the hands of God as He delights in seeing us launched over and over into His will and purpose for our life. This reminds me of Zephaniah 3:17:

> *The LORD your God is with you, he is mighty to save. He will take great delight in you, he will quiet you with his love, he will rejoice over you with singing.*

Taking It Personally

Do I know that Jesus is real simply because it is documented in the Bible? Does my belief come only from all of the above-noted facts concerning His birth, His life, and His death on the cross? It is true that information strengthens my faith in Him. But there's more. I know Jesus is real because of what has happened in my life since I invited Him in. It's been 25 years, and since that time I've never again experienced that void, that inner vacuum. There is no reason to scratch because the itch is gone.

My brother once said, "When Bunny changed, I knew there was a Christ!" People who were acquainted with me before my personal encounter with the living God can attest to the fact that I am now a different person. The anger, bitterness, sarcasm, and low self-image have vanished, leaving behind someone who is at peace with herself and others. I'm often amazed when people refer to me as thoughtful, considerate, and kind. This has not been the result of a conscious effort, but of a transformation that comes from an intimate walk with Jesus. I have a peace that passes all understanding and a contentment beyond compare.

If you haven't already asked Jesus to come into your life, please take the time to do so right now. Simply admit that you are a sinner in need of a Savior. Acknowledge that Jesus died on the cross for your sins and rose from the dead on the third day. Then ask Him to come into your life. You may not feel anything at first, but based on God's Word, that confession is your passport into eternal life. And in time, you, too, will notice a transformation that is more glorious than anything you could possibly imagine.*

---

* If you have decided to make that decision, please write and tell me about it. I will respond. I want to encourage you in your new walk in Christ. My address is P. O. Box 2601, Pasadena, CA 91102.

> *I know Jesus is real because of what has happened in my life since I invited Him in. It's been 25 years, and since that time I've never again experienced that void, that inner vacuum.*

Applying the Seven Secrets

Our youngest daughter has taught me many lessons. My husband, Frank, and I together have five grown children and an eight-year-old "surprise." When Gabrielle introduces herself, she usually mentions that she is a piano player. Her gift of music manifested itself before she was two years old, and her delight in playing is quickly made evident to anyone who visits our home. Once guests arrive, it usually takes only about 60 seconds for her to get them in the room with the piano to listen to one of her carefully practiced pieces. She has performed in many recitals and shows great potential. With all our other children grown or in college, Gabrielle is the center of attention, receiving endless praise for her musical accomplishments.

That would explain the jolting experience she had when we hosted a reception at our home for about 30 people. After we had eaten, we asked a good friend, who is an extraordinary pianist and soloist, to perform for us. You could see the expressions of awe on our guests' faces as she began to perform the beautiful song "We Shall Behold Him." There were oohs and aahs, and several people were wiping away tears.

One of them was Gabrielle. About halfway through the song, she approached me with tears streaming down her face. For a moment I wondered if they were tears of joy, but the expression on her face said differently.

"What's wrong, Gabrielle?" I asked her, feeling deep concern.

She leaned over and whispered, "The devil is trying to tell me this woman plays better than me! Would you flick him off my shoulder?"

What a shock for Gabrielle! The truth was that our friend did indeed play the piano better than she did. And we can all glean a great spiritual lesson from my daughter's disillusionment. In order to practice the seven spiritual factors in this book, we not only have to deal with our mind and flesh, but we also have to battle with the devil. He can be counted on not only to taunt us in our weaknesses, but to inspire unholy pride in our strengths.

The devil will also attempt to restrain us from taking that "one big step" so that many small steps will not follow. The big step I'm talking about is laying down all preconceived notions and opinions and acknowledging Jesus as Savior and Lord. Only then can He make Himself real in our lives; only then can we apply His proven principles every day.

Next, we need to make the Bible our final authority and take the Lord at His Word—and with every ounce of our being apply His truths to each situation we find ourselves in. We don't just fall into this. It takes a daily concerted effort, and we have to stick with it, no matter how difficult the trial.

Do you find in your single or married life feelings of discouragement, disillusionment, or confusion? Do waves of frustration, sometimes even anger, hang over you like a soaked blanket? Wouldn't you like to leave behind life's heaviest weights and soar to the heights for which you were designed? Are you sick and tired of being sick and tired? Do you feel as if you are constantly taking two steps forward and three steps back (and that's on a good day)? Are you earthbound in your view of heavenly things? Then let me challenge you to make the decision to live your life God's way. You'll never be the same.

Obedience Is Better Than Sacrifice

When I was a new believer, trying to grow in grace, countless books and tapes—not to mention innumerable scriptures—seemed to be pulling me in a hundred different directions. I so wanted to do the right thing and make the right decisions in my life. But I didn't know where to start.

Just today I received a call from a sincere Christian woman who said she was waiting with much anticipation for this book to be released. She was my hostess at a women's conference I spoke at and seemed to hang on every word I said. By the time I was ready to leave town, her husband said she had been miraculously transformed.

Unfortunately, her telephone call revealed to me that she had fallen back into some of her old patterns. And she seemed to think that the solution to changing was to acquire new information. Just for the record, please bear in mind that this book is more about "applied" principles than new ideas. Much of what you read you have probably heard before in one form or another. It's important to remember that spirituality is not based on how much knowledge you have acquired, but rather on how you personally apply that knowledge.

Let's take the challenge to live our lives God's way!

My recommendation to the woman was to write a letter recounting everything she had learned when I was with her, to read the correspondence herself, and then to begin practicing it all again. "To obey is better than sacrifice" (1 Samuel 15:22) is a scripture which needs to be burned into our hearts.

But please don't get the idea that I'm writing this book because I am always perfectly obedient to the Bible and have somehow managed to reach Christian perfection. I'm not, I haven't, and it is unlikely that you will be either while living on this planet. But I would like to challenge you as the Apostle Paul admonished us when he said, "Follow my example, as I follow the example of Christ" (1 Corinthians 11:1).

So with God's command for obedience firmly planted in our minds, I'd like to invite you on a trip. I want us to walk together along a path which may seem long at times, but boasts of wonders that will appear around every bend. Let's take the challenge to live our lives God's way. The journey is not as long nor the task as difficult as many would imagine—and we will never be the same! It does, however, require one giant step—a straightforward decision to go forward. That giant step will be followed by consistent obedience in what may appear to be small, insignificant "baby" steps. It is this step-by-step process that will lift us out of whatever snares may have entangled us. And as we adhere to the process, aligning our base with God's will, eventually we will soar to new heights. Just like Gabrielle's toy was intended to do, we will learn to fly, soaring on eagles' wings as God intended us to do.

Chapter One Workbook

Reflection:

Is the Bible the *final* authority in your life? That means no excuses, no alibis, and no justifications. The goal is to do it God's way no matter what. Have you or are you ready to make that commitment?

Meditation:

Scripture Memory:
"To obey is better than sacrifice"
(1 Samuel 15:22).

Response:

Document how this chapter has spoken to you.

2
The Long and Winding Road

Help me to know Wisdom...

No two women who read this book will be at the exact same place in their lives, because no two spiritual journeys are alike. However, even though the routes may differ, the destination for every Christian is identical. Once we overcome the obstacles that face us in this life, we'll stand victorious before Jesus!

But how can we be assured of a successful journey? We can move forward confidently because we don't have to go alone. Besides the fact that Jesus walks with us every step (or baby step) of the way, there will be someone else calling out to us at each fork in the road—someone I know you'll want to meet. She needs to be introduced because she will be an indispensable companion to us on our journey.

A Meeting at the Crossroads

Practicing the seven spiritual secrets and putting them to work in our lives requires daily direction. Whenever we have a decision to make, we need to know which way to go.

Whether our dilemma involves spending money or saving money, selecting a mate or staying single, making a decision about having children or cultivating the children we already have, nurturing or ending a relationship, traveling across town or taking a luxury cruise around the world, we are constantly faced with decisions. And it is the quality of our choices that directs the course of our future.

My brother, Pastor Cliff Ashe, says, "We are often only one decision away from disaster." And I'm sure you agree with him when you think about the lives of certain people you know. One bad choice can devastate someone's whole life. But I'm not worried, and you shouldn't be either. Instead, I'm excited about our future because God's Word teaches us that we have a very well-qualified escort for our journey. Her name is Wisdom.

Let me encourage you to stop reading this book for a few minutes and read the eighth chapter of Proverbs. Here is an excerpt:

> *Does not wisdom call out?...On the heights along*
> *the way, where the paths meet, she takes her*
> *stand; beside the gates leading into the city, at*
> *the entrances, she cries aloud: "To you, O men, I*
> *call out; I raise my voice to all mankind. You who*
> *are simple, gain prudence; you who are foolish,*
> *gain understanding. Listen, for I have worthy*
> *things to say..." (verses 1-6).*

When we first read this passage, we may not think it applies to us because we don't consider ourselves simple or foolish. But let me assure you—once we get a good look at ourselves in the light of God's Word, it shouldn't take us long to realize that we are both.

> *God's Word teaches us that we have a very well-qualified escort for our journey. Her name is Wisdom.*

Please notice that Wisdom *stands* where the paths meet (crossroads) and at the entrance of the city gates. Both of these places represent congested areas. Even though anyone can come *to* the city gate, not all can *go through*. Wisdom stands at the entrance before anything or anyone is turned back. And what is she doing there? She is crying aloud: "To you, O men, I call out; I raise my voice to all mankind" (Proverbs 8:4).

So why do we have to seek Wisdom? After all, she *cries aloud.* The challenge to us is that Wisdom is not the only one calling out. At a crossroads or an entrance to a city, there is much activity. It is difficult to hear a single voice because of all the noise.

Have you ever become separated from a child or a friend at an amusement park or shopping mall? Our first reactions are usually confusion and panic. What a great relief to hear his or her familiar voice or laughter rise above the other people's clamor. How grateful we are to catch a glimpse of that person in the distance. Would you recognize Wisdom crying out in a crowd? Maybe not, because recognizing her doesn't just happen. We have to become familiar with the sound of her voice.

I'd like to compare the "entrance of the city" to any place where we are first confronted by a new situation or circumstance. We say we've "come to a crossroads" at those times when we are about to make a final decision. That's when we need Wisdom the most.

And that's when our friend Wisdom stands and cries out for us to find her and to listen to her. But all around her are thoughts and feelings, which are also chattering at us. Some are even yelling. One very loud voice is Deception, whom we almost never see because it dresses in a way that seems to blend in with the surroundings. Deception is pleasant to the eyes, and its voice is soothing in the midst of the confusion. That soothing voice tempts us to walk with it.

It's really not hard to identify Deception, however. Unlike Wisdom, Deception usually approaches us. And the tricky part is that it can impersonate Wisdom's voice. Have you ever heard an impersonator? If you listen long enough, he or she runs out of material and the person's voice returns to its original state. That is why I love the anonymous quote, "Patience is the weapon which forces deceit to reveal itself."

Even though Wisdom is standing and calling, we may miss her if we are carried away in the crowd by Confusion, Lies, and Self-pity, not to mention the well-intentioned but sometimes wrong advice of friends or associates. Wisdom has a fixed position, so we must proceed slowly so as not to pass her. Our ears have to be attuned to her voice. Isn't it comforting to know that she is waiting for us? There is nothing we are facing in our lives that she cannot handle.

But how can we find Wisdom? The first step is acknowledging that she exists and wants to be found. Second, it is necessary to spend time training our ears so we will know her. Let me suggest that you begin in the book of Proverbs, which was written by King Solomon, the wisest man on earth. There are 31 chapters of Proverbs. Begin reading a chapter a day and connect it to the day of the month. For example, if today is the tenth day of the month, then begin with Proverbs, the tenth chapter. If you miss a day or two, go to the corresponding day and read that chapter. Reading Proverbs month after month sensitizes our ears to Wisdom.

But perhaps you're thinking, "Look, Bunny, I have some real problems right here, right now! I can't wait for months to address the situations facing me. What can I do?"

Proverbs 11:14 says, "...in the multitude of counsellors there is safety" (KJV). Until you can discern the voice of Wisdom for yourself, it would be wise to seek counsel from others who are in a close and balanced walk with Jesus (more about that in chapters 10 and 11). The Bible will be their final authority, and God will give you peace with their instruction. Even when we can identify Wisdom, a godly friend or counselor is invaluable before we make our final decision. Deception is cunning, and a wise advisor can help us to recognize his disguise.

The Voice of Wisdom

Now that we have acknowledged that Wisdom is standing and crying out to us in the crowds of life, it's important for us to know something about her so we can recognize her voice. Where did she come from, and why does she care about us? Our answers are still found in the eighth chapter of Proverbs. Let me draw your attention to verses 22 through 30 as Wisdom describes herself:

> *The LORD brought me forth as the first of his works, before his deeds of old; I was appointed from eternity, from the beginning, before the world began. When there were no oceans, I was given birth, when there were no springs abounding with water; before the mountains were settled in place, before the hills, I was given birth, before he*

made the earth or its fields or any of the dust of the world. I was there when he set the heavens in place, when he marked out the horizon on the face of the deep, when he established the clouds above and fixed securely the fountains of the deep, when he gave the sea its boundary so the waters would not overstep his command, and when he marked out the foundations of the earth. Then I was the craftsman at his side. I was filled with delight day after day, rejoicing always in his presence, rejoicing in his whole world and delighting in mankind.

Wow! Wisdom was there when God formed the earth; she was a "craftsman at his side." It's interesting that we don't find Wisdom next to God, announcing her right to expound great knowledge and understanding. She possesses both qualities, but when she is with God we find her simply "rejoicing in His presence." She is an instrument of God who is excited about our potential. That gives us another clue for recognizing her. Wisdom is not Wisdom if she is forever talking about herself. Her truths will always lead us toward rejoicing in God and away from personal recognition.

Wisdom passionately wants us to find her because we are her delight. She most assuredly is pleased by how God has designed us—by our individual uniqueness, by the various gifts we have, and by the wonderful truth that we are created in the image of God. No wonder she wants to spend time with us. But are we excited about being with her? I don't know about you, but I am. Let's search the crowd and find her.

> *Wisdom is an instrument of God who is excited about our potential.*

It doesn't take us long to discover that it's going to take time to find Wisdom. There is so much movement and activity in our lives. But once she is found, she will be easier and easier to discern each time we need her. By now, whatever we are dealing with in life should take a backseat to our pursuit for Wisdom. That means when we're confronted by a situation or problem, our best response is, at least temporarily, no response. If the decision involves another person, we need to let them know we'll get back to them. Because how can we respond when we haven't spoken to Wisdom?

What are our criteria in identifying Wisdom? Proverbs 8:6-8 will be our guide, as Wisdom tells us about herself:

> *Listen, for I have worthy things to say; I open my lips to speak what is right. My mouth speaks what is true, for my lips detest wickedness. All the words of my mouth are just; none of them is crooked or perverse (emphasis added).*

Whatever Wisdom says will be right, true, and just. Of course, some people may contend that those three points are relative to our time and culture. That might apply to some people, but not for those of us believers who are traveling down the road called eternal life on our way home to heaven. We recognize the Bible as our final word. Still, we have to be taught correctly. Wisdom instructs in Proverbs 8, verses 10 and 11:

> *Choose my instruction instead of silver, knowledge rather than choice gold,* for wisdom is more precious than rubies, and nothing you desire can compare with her *(emphasis added).*

What are your desires in life? This is a great time to make a list and check it twice. Maybe you want to retire by the time you are 35 years old. Or perhaps it's your dream to get married and have children. Maybe you've got a craving for a new house and a fancier mode of transportation. It could be that your mind is fixed on a college education, a great vacation, a recreational vehicle, money in the bank, a good credit rating, new clothes, or a face-lift. You get the picture. Can you see Wisdom looking over your shoulder and smiling? No matter what you list, *nothing* can compare to finding her. Look at what happens when she is in our possession:

> *I love those who love me, and those who seek*
> *me find me. With me are riches and honor,*
> *enduring wealth and prosperity. My fruit is better*
> *than fine gold; what I yield surpasses choice silver.*
> *I walk in the way of righteousness, along the*
> *paths of justice, bestowing wealth on those who*
> *love me and making their treasuries full*
> *(Proverbs 8:17-21).*

What a relief! We have been running in a hundred different directions with our miscellaneous pursuits. Meanwhile, Wisdom says that when we have her, we have it all. But we must "search for her as hidden treasure." Once I realized Wisdom was looking for me in the crowd, desiring to fellowship with me and to impart her knowledge, I was thrilled! The pursuit of Wisdom, I decided, would be my lifelong quest.

We meet Wisdom everywhere we turn. In each decision, no matter how small or big, she is there. No wonder James 1:19 teaches, "be quick to listen, slow to speak." We must pause to get direction. And those forks in the road happen constantly throughout the day. Each conversation, response, and decision takes us one way or another. Are we headed in the direction in which we want to go? Did we pause to consult Wisdom? Isn't it better for us to say nothing at all than to blurt out a response or quickly move toward a conclusion without her?

How refreshing it is to sit beside the road of life watching Impatience, Confusion, and Chaos rush by. Wisdom meets us where we are and leads us to where we need to be. But that requires patience on our part. It is much easier to jump up and make something happen than to rest in the knowledge that she has everything under control.

And what happens when we finally meet Wisdom? Do we stand in the middle of the street straining to hear her speak?

Finding Our Way Home

Once we have found Wisdom, we can expect her to put her arms around us and lead us away from the "madding crowd." Proverbs 9:1-6 describes where she is taking us:

> *Wisdom has built her house; she has hewn out its seven pillars. She has prepared her meat and mixed her wine; she has also set her table. She has sent out her maids, and she calls from the highest point of the city. "Let all who are simple come in here!" she says to those who lack judgment. "Come, eat my food and drink the wine I have mixed. Leave your simple ways and you will live; walk in the way of understanding."*

Wisdom takes us to her house to partake of her hospitality. It is there that we meet her roommates: "I, wisdom, dwell together with prudence; I possess knowledge and discretion" (Proverbs 8:12).

Webster's Dictionary defines wisdom as "a wise attitude or course of action; judgment."

Wisdom "dwells with prudence." Prudence is "the ability to govern and discipline oneself by the use of reason."

They are joined by Knowledge, which is "the fact or condition of knowing something with familiarity gained through experience or association."

And let's not forget Discretion, which is "cautious reserve in speech."

Now that we've come home with Wisdom, we can relax in her hospitality and with her friends. Confusion, Doubt, Fear, and Anxiety are not welcome guests here, even though they want very much to visit. It's just as well they aren't invited—they would feel very uncomfortable in an environment where their shortcomings were exposed, their deceit revealed. They'll wait outside, though, hoping we get distracted and wander away from that place of safety. I've done that on many occasions, and paid a dear price.

Be quick to hear and slow to speak.

Our fellowship with Wisdom will be so rich we won't want to leave. She'll be included in the work to be done in our families, vocation, or ministry. Once we have been to Wisdom's home, it won't be necessary to meet her at the city gates again. We'll now know the way back to her.

Wisdom says in Proverbs 8:34-35:

> *Blessed is the man who listens to me, watching daily at my doors, waiting at my doorway. For*

*whoever finds me finds life and receives favor
from the* LORD.

How many unanswered questions do you have? How
many perplexing situations are you facing? As you can see
from Proverbs 8, the answers are completely available. They
are possessed by Wisdom, and she longs to give us her guidance. But we must pursue her. We must want the relationship.

But why is it that we hear so few conversations about
Wisdom? Why is her name so seldom mentioned? Why does
the world seem to lack the passionate pursuit to find her?
It's true; she appears to be a very well-kept secret. I think I
know the reason, because I avoided her myself for so many
years. I was forever plowing ahead into the future, figuring
things out as I went, making rash decisions, then constantly
asking God to fix my unnecessary mistakes. That's what I was
doing while I was ignoring Wisdom. And believe me, my
friend, it's no way to live.

Let's stop right now and meditate on what we've just
learned. Soon you'll approach a fork in the road. It will
require your interaction with someone on the telephone, a
person riding on a bus, someone you meet standing in a line,
a coworker, or perhaps it will be a friend, a loved one, or a
family member. You'll need Wisdom. But how should you
relate to her? How does she become real in your life?
Proverbs 7:4 instructs: "Say to wisdom, 'You are my sister,'
and call understanding your kinsman....'"

By way of illustration, let me tell you about one of my
own sisters. Her name is Elenor, but we call her Bootsie. She
was given that nickname because when she was little, she
used to walk around the house in my father's boots. When
we were growing up, she was always there. We lived in the
same house and, as little children, we slept in the same bed.

She used to say to my mother, "Mommy, please don't make me sleep with Bunny!" This was because of my sleeping habits. All through the night, I would incessantly rock back and forth in my sleep. And because I liked the feel of certain fabrics, I was constantly moving my fingers. It drove her crazy!

Today Bootsie and I are close friends. I love her and thoroughly enjoy her company. During conversations with other people, it is natural for me to recognize her presence, and I readily listen to what she has to say. As a matter of fact, it would be rude if I did not give her the courtesy of responding to her comments in our discussions.

Well, according to God's Word, Wisdom is also my sister. The difference is that she never leaves my side. She is there to give me direction at every turn, with every decision, with every choice, and in every conversation. But because I cannot see her, it is necessary for me to consciously remember her presence. She has the ability to allow me to hear what people are saying as well as what they are not saying. She is able to show me their hearts, to discern their spirits. So if someone asked me a question and I blurted out the answer without pausing to hear Wisdom's voice, wouldn't that be foolish on my part? Of course it would.

Instead, when I relate to Wisdom as my sister who is always there and has all of the answers, her presence immediately calms me. At times, I reach over and take her unseen hand to remind myself that she is there. At last I can stop trying to figure everything out. I can become a listener instead of a talker. I can understand the discretion of being "quick to hear and slow to speak" because it's not just me listening or responding any longer. Wisdom's presence can become as real to me as that of my earthly sister.

When you are having a conversation with someone, let Wisdom direct your attention to the person with whom you are talking and then to your response. You'll notice that the direction she gives will come from what you have learned in God's Word.

> *Wisdom has the ability to allow me to hear what people are saying as well as what they are not saying. She is able to show me their hearts, to discern their spirits.*

Doesn't it give you peace knowing you are not alone? Doesn't it comfort you that Wisdom knows everything about the people you are talking to and also knows just what they need to hear and how you should respond? As we close this chapter, it is with great pleasure that I end with a written guarantee from God concerning your ability to find and obtain Wisdom. James 1:5-8 says:

> *If any of you lacks wisdom, he should ask God, who gives generously to all without finding fault, and it will be given to him. But when he asks, he must believe and not doubt, because he who doubts is like a wave of the sea, blown and tossed by the wind. That man should not think he will receive anything from the Lord; he is a double-minded man, unstable in all he does.*

You see? We are not alone; we have a friend. Let's take time to be a friend to our friend, a sister to our sister, God's wonderful gift to us—Wisdom. Wisdom is ours for the asking. And she'll go with us willingly and joyfully as we move forward in our pursuit of the Seven Secrets.

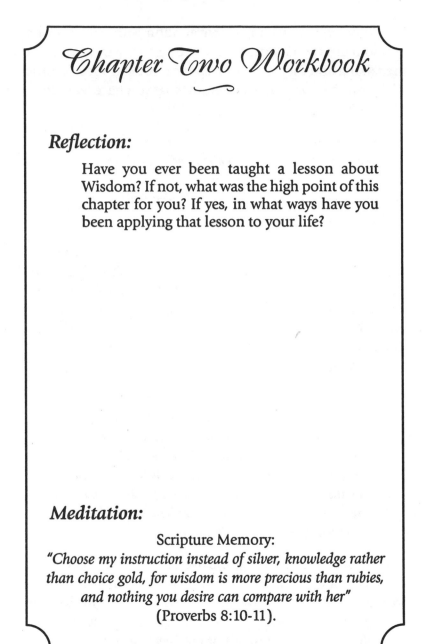

Chapter Two Workbook

Reflection:

Have you ever been taught a lesson about Wisdom? If not, what was the high point of this chapter for you? If yes, in what ways have you been applying that lesson to your life?

Meditation:

Scripture Memory:
"Choose my instruction instead of silver, knowledge rather than choice gold, for wisdom is more precious than rubies, and nothing you desire can compare with her"
(Proverbs 8:10-11).

Response:

Today, practice feeling Wisdom's presence throughout the day, in meetings, personal conversations, and decisions. Record your experiences.

3

Oh, No, Not That Again!

I choose to be submitted...

According to the Bible, submission to God is the beginning of wisdom. Recently I was invited to speak at an exclusive luncheon for businesswomen which was attended by lawyers, doctors, and an array of other professionals. The subject of my message was submission. And, as usual, my message caused quite a stir.

If you're familiar with my other books, you may be thinking, "Come on, Bunny, enough is enough. What more can you say about submission?"

It's true. I've talked about this before. You may remember my book *Liberated Through Submission*, which has been a very controversial publication ever since its release. I've talked about this very important subject in other books as well. But please don't skip this chapter thinking you've already heard all I have to say about submission! Unless you have perfected the principle, there are still some things to be learned.

When I first mentioned the word "submission" at the businesswomen's luncheon, some of the ladies in attendance looked as if they had been slapped in the face. But they soon changed their minds. Whether I'm speaking to a Christian or non-Christian audience, the message of submission invariably rings true. By the time the luncheon ended, many of those professional women gladly received my book. Why? Because submission is not only a Christian principle, it is a universal principle.

I was recently interviewed on a general market radio station about this topic. It is not unusual for secular media to deny that the Bible is the Word of God. Yet the opportunity to be heard by thousands of unbelievers was thrilling to me. Bob, the talk show host, informed me that their radio station had advertised the program heavily. And he warned me that a lot of people were already waiting for the phone lines to open up.

Once Bob had introduced me, he immediately jumped in with an inflammatory question, "So, Bunny, you've come on the air today to teach wives that they have to submit to their husbands, haven't you?"

Amused, I replied, "No, Bob, I'm here today to tell everyone listening that you're a submitted man."

"How so?" he asked, sounding a little puzzled.

"Well, *Webster's Dictionary* defines the word 'submit' as 'to yield,' which is voluntary. Tell me something, Bob, do you own this radio station?"

"No."

"Do you have a general manager?"

"Yes."

"Do you always agree with the programming assigned to you?"

"Of course not."

"Then the very fact I'm speaking to you today means you are a submitted man."

Bob burst into laughter and replied, "I guess you're right!"

> *Submission is not only a Christian principle,*
> *it is a universal principle.*

We conversed for a little while longer on the subject, then he opened up the telephone lines. The first caller had obviously been waiting for that moment because she announced emphatically, "Hello, Bunny-bimbo! I'll tell you what—they need to take your book and burn it in a fire!"

Refusing to be disturbed by her outburst, I asked her how she defined submission. She equated it with subservience, physical abuse, and being asked to do something immoral. I explained that submission has gotten a bad name because it has been defined incorrectly and applied improperly.

Then I inquired, "Did you know that feminists are submitted women?"

Harriett sounded as if she were gnawing on the telephone. Undaunted, I continued, "Many feminist groups have an organizational flow chart. When the board meets to make decisions for their organization, some of the members may disagree, but everyone knows the president has the right to make the final decision. Before they leave that room, those in disagreement must *graciously submit* because they know a 'house divided against itself cannot stand.'"

I'm not sure Harriett changed her mind, but at least she heard me.

The reality is that everyone submits to somebody. It's never a question of "do you submit," but rather, "To whom are you submitted?" As Christian believers, it is essential for us to accept God's Word as our organizational flow chart, whether we are male or female, single or married. We are always answerable to someone. That's God's way of directing us into being answerable to Him.

Let's also keep in mind that the caller was also under the misconception that submission includes physical abuse and yielding to immoral acts. *It does not.*

Not long ago, the Southern Baptists were raked across the coals for writing in their charter the statement, "Wives must submit to their husbands." They recanted, and I was sorry because in fact they had been right. But they erred in not applying the principle of submission to everyone: male, female, single, and married.

As we've seen, the married woman *is* called to submit to her husband. But she's not the only person called to submission. Every Christian husband is instructed to submit to God by loving his wife as Christ loved the church (see Ephesians 5:25), by living with her according to understanding, as well as by being the final decision-maker and the spiritual leader in his home. All Christians are to be in submission, including single men and women who are directed to submit to their parents, the government, their pastors, and their employers.

The principle of submission must be taught in its entirety or it will continue to be ridiculed by both secular society and the church. When the Southern Baptist convention platform singled out the married woman only, public appreciation for a clear biblical explanation of submission was doomed—at least temporarily. Fortunately it burns bright in many an understanding heart. But in countless churches, it remains a well-guarded secret.

> *The principle of submission must be taught in its entirety or it will continue to be ridiculed by both secular society and the church.*

The Broken Traffic Signal

In my book *Knight in Shining Armor*, which was written for Christian singles who would like to find a godly mate, I give an example that bears repeating. It helps to illustrate the simplicity of submission as a powerful principle.

Before you drive your car to a destination, you probably don't pray, "Lord, whatever You do, please don't let there be a broken traffic signal at a busy intersection on the way to where I am going!"

Why don't we pray that prayer? Because we've learned by taking driver's education classes or by reading the driver's handbook that when we come to an intersection and the traffic signal is broken, the first thing we have to do is *stop*. We allow the cars on the right to proceed first. After they go, the process is continued until the traffic signal is repaired. Now, what if that kind of system had not been established before any of us learned to drive? There would be utter chaos at the intersection, with people arguing and bumping into each other, each trying to prove that he or she has the right-of-way.

Why do you think God initiated the principle of submission? One possible explanation is He knew that He had created free-thinking individuals, and that by nature every person does what is right in his or her own eyes. He could foresee that if any two people spent any amount of time together, sooner or later their communication would collapse. The "signal" would become broken. If a system wasn't already established, there would be utter confusion in the relationship.

Unfortunately, many believers do not understand the principle of submission, and their relationships are filled with anger and confusion. As a judge once said, "Ignorance of the law does not excuse us from the penalty of the law."

Since most of us would agree that submission applies to marriage, let's use a different example to illustrate how the principle works in another very familiar situation. Let's suppose an employer gives a Christian man an assignment with which he does not agree. He feels strongly that his boss's idea is a waste of time. Does he go to the lunchroom and complain to his colleagues about the assignment and his boss? If so, that Christian man would be disobeying Philippians 2:14-15, which says:

> *Do everything without complaining or arguing, so that you may become blameless and pure, children of God without fault in a crooked and depraved generation, in which you shine like stars in the universe....*

According to Paul's words, a believer should never be heard complaining or arguing. Does that mean we as Christians are supposed to let people walk all over us? No, the proper procedure works just like the rule for the broken traffic signal, allowing all to pass through with no confusion or chaos.

Four Steps into Submission

Should an employee's boss make what appears to be an unreasonable request, the first thing the employee should do is *stop*. He will need time to collect his thoughts, allow Wisdom to assert herself in order to keep himself from reacting emotionally by saying and doing something foolish.

The next step is for him to *speak the truth.* You may say, "Well, that won't be hard!" It may be harder than you think, if it's done according to Ephesians 4:15. God's Word says we should "speak the truth *in love.*" I was fired from three jobs because I aggressively spoke the truth—not in love, but in anger and frustration. God's love is unconditional—no strings attached. When the man in our example shares the truth *in love,* he will say exactly what he's thinking with the right tone of voice, facial expressions, and gestures.

If his employer does not agree with him, the man's next step will be to *submit* (yield) and to give the issue to God.

Submission is a uniquely powerful principle because it operates on faith, and "without faith it is impossible to please God" (Hebrews 11:6). It takes faith to believe that God knows all, hears all, and will intervene on our behalf without any further input from us. It means we believe that He can communicate into the hearts and minds of our employers (whether they are saved or unsaved) or whomever it is that stands in a position of authority over us. God is able to lead earthly authorities in the right direction. And He doesn't need our help in doing so.

After Jesus died on the cross for our sins, God could have written in His Word, "If you confess with your mouth and believe in your heart that God has raised Him from the dead, you shall be saved. The End." God could have left us here to deal with life and the devil on our own, not really getting involved with us until we've died and gone to heaven. The very fact that He cares about everything we do is an incredible blessing. However, we have to allow Him to intervene to reap the reward. Here's a motto worth memorizing:

Submission means God intervenes.

If you are married, the same four steps apply in your home. Sharing the truth in love will allow God to use you as an effective "helper" in your husband's life (see Genesis 2:18). Many married women attempt to sweep controversial issues under the rug in the name of peace. That puts lumps in the carpet, and after awhile neither spouse is able to walk through the relationship without tripping!

The last step is to *wait* on God to demonstrate what *His* will is concerning the situation. Notice I said *His will* and not who is right or wrong. Sometimes we can have all the facts correct, but the conclusion still is not His will.

Think about the man in our previous example. It will utterly stagger the imagination of his employer as he watches his employee, with a cheerful heart and attitude, tackle a project to which he's outspokenly opposed. The man has stopped, lovingly made his position clear, and his boss knows they don't agree. Now, that Christian man's pleasant behavior speaks volumes about his relationship with the Lord.

But what if someone's employer or pastor or, in the case of marriage, husband, makes a really terrible decision? The real question is not "if" but "when." No one is perfect, and mistakes are inevitable. However, when we operate according to the principle of submission, mistakes become blessings. Faith tells us we worship a God who can "hit a straight line with a crooked stick."

Mistakes give us the opportunity to remind the person who committed the error, "Because I am a Christian, I submitted to your decision peacefully. I still believe God can lead you in the way you should go. I also believe that if you make a mistake, God can fix it. Now what can I do to help?"

When people who are in authority in our lives make a mistake and we are there to help them fix it, that expression of kindness allows them to accept what they did as being wrong instead of needing to justify it or blame it on someone else. It also endears us to that person because, as Jesus explained, we have not condemned them. The next time we give our opinion, we can be sure the person will give it more consideration because we have earned the right to be heard.

Submission works the same in marriage as in our single lives. If you're single and you're paying attention, you'll have plenty of practice in the four steps of submission. You will be dealing with your parents, pastors, employers, law enforcement officers, and government officials long before you ever consider marriage.

A Dose of My Own Medicine

When my daughter Launi was planning her wedding to our wonderful son-in-law Jason, I made her promise she would faithfully send out thank-you notes for the wedding gifts they received. She solemnly swore to be diligent in that area, knowing it was very important to me. But months after the ceremony, a few of our relatives and friends started questioning me as to whether Launi and Jason had received their gift.

Of course I was upset. I couldn't dial my daughter's number fast enough. When I confronted her with her obvious lack of diligence, she responded, "I'm sorry, Mom, but Jason said he wanted me to wait until he had time to sit down with me and do it together. So in *submission* to my husband, I waited."

Of course there was silence on my end. She had me; she'd given me a dose of my own medicine. I couldn't help but smile. I encouraged Launi to remind her husband that it is very important to follow through on thank-you notes and hung up the telephone. Even though the cards weren't yet in the mail, I rejoiced in knowing that my daughter understood and was practicing submission. One of the greatest blessings of practicing submission is seeing it emulated in our children.

Lessons in Patience

An important ingredient necessary for a successfully submitted life is patience. And yet patience is something that is sorely lacking in most of us because it requires us to release our control over a situation. We have to believe that God will intervene when we are called to submit to someone in authority. But that means He'll do it according to His timetable, not ours. And that means waiting.

Time and time again, I have counseled with women who are in the workplace and really want to return home and raise their children. All too often their husbands don't agree, and that puts these women in a difficult position.

A day in the life of a woman like this may sound familiar to you. She wakes up early and rushes to get the children ready to drop off at daycare or school. She spends eight hours at work, finishing only in time to pick the children up from school or—worse yet—to have her children already returned home to an empty house. Once she gets home, there is dinner to fix, homework to tend to, baths to supervise, and, finally, the bittersweet pleasure of tucking the kids into bed, realizing she's had almost no quality time with them at all. Meanwhile the house has to be kept somewhat tidy, the laundry done, the bills paid, and, unfortunately, oftentimes there is far too little assistance from her spouse.

There is no way to count the number of women who have sat across from me in my living room and cried over living out this very set of circumstances. They just can't seem to get their husbands to understand how difficult it is for them to work outside the home. There's no question that many families need a second paycheck to make ends meet. And when these stressed-out women talk with me, I can understand why they don't like my advice. Nonetheless, I always tell them, "You must submit to your husband's decision. Go to God with the problem, and be patient with Him while He works out the answer."

I suggest that they meet with their husbands and clearly state their reasons for wanting to stay home. There is no need for tears or tantrums; just a simple statement is all it takes. It could be on the order of, "Honey, I know I've nagged you in the past about quitting my job, but I'm not going to do that again. As a matter of fact, I won't be bringing it up anymore at all. But if you'll permit me to say one last thing, it's this: I love you and my heart's desire is to come home from my job so I can better serve you and the children."

From that day forward, this woman should do her very best at work and at home. There may be times when she'll cry from being exhausted, but she reminds herself to do everything "as unto the Lord." Women who take this course often report experiencing an emotional release because they believe by faith that God is working on their behalf. They are able to trust Him, even if everything seems to be pointing in the wrong direction.

I have never seen one case where the woman followed that course of action and remained in the workplace. Sometimes it has taken as long as a year for change to come, and her patience may have been stretched to the limit, but it did happen.

Scripture teaches that God's desire is for wives to be "keepers at home" (Titus 2:5), and it's difficult to do that without being *at* home. It's important for a wife to do things

God's way. That's why I advise women to yield to their husbands' authority and then get out of God's way.

When my sister-in-law, Audree, gave her heart to the Lord, she hit the ground running. I don't think I've ever met a new believer who has equaled her passion for God. She quickly grasped the importance of being a keeper of the home and shared with my brother, Cliff, her desire to leave the workplace. Cliff, who at that time was a corporate executive, found that the primary challenge was that Audree's income equaled his, and they needed her contribution to make ends meet. But Audree had faith that God would provide, and Cliff consented. Within a week he was promoted at work and making twice the salary he'd previously been making.

New Marriage, New Perspective

Sandra is the owner and president of a real estate company. She has a host of agents working for her, and it took a lot of blood, sweat, and tears for her to reach that position. When she was a single woman, she was perfectly happy to work around the clock, but once she married the man of her dreams that all changed. It was suddenly imperative that she reduce her hours at work. And in actuality, Sandra didn't mind the adjustment. Instead, she had a different challenge. How could she step from a place of leadership at work into a place of submission once she left the job? At the office, she was the final decision-maker. At home, she wasn't.

At first, in the blush of a new marriage, she welcomed the difference. But as time went on, it became more and more irritating. Sandra was used to making snap decisions, and her husband seemed to take forever in coming to any conclusion at all. His slow response was beginning to drive her crazy. Finally Sandra confided in Mae, a godly woman at her church who understood the principle of submission.

"Sandra," Mae smiled, "you don't need to change hats when you come home. You need to keep wearing the same hat."

"What do you mean? Of course I have to change hats. I'm a boss at work and a wife at home. Those are two different hats!"

Mae then asked a very penetrating question. "Who really owns your company?"

The answer immediately shot back from Sandra. "I do."

When Mae didn't respond and gave her a quizzical look, Sandra searched her mind for another answer. She chuckled when she realized what her counselor was getting at. "Well, okay, even though I said I owned the company, I know it's really God who is the CEO. As a matter of fact, that was important to me when I set up the corporation. I dedicated everything I was doing to the Lord."

"Then who owns your company?" Mae once again questioned.

Smiling, Sandra replied, "God does."

Sandra confirmed that she prayed about every decision before it was made and tried to follow in the direction of the Lord's leading. She also admitted that, at times, she probably didn't wait on God for answers as long as she should. "Sometimes I have to ask the Lord to undo the messes I make when I jump ahead of Him."

Mae sat quietly and watched Sandra intently. She could see her friend processing the information.

Finally, Sandra announced, "Oh, I get it! I'm submitted to God at work and submitted to God at home through my husband. That's what you meant when you said it's the same hat!"

Mae laughed out loud. "That's right, Sandra, nothing changes. And you know that God doesn't always give you quick answers when you need to make a decision at work. So why should you demand that from your husband?"

Sandra shook her head.

Mae continued, "The Scripture teaches, 'Whatever you do in word or deed, do all to the glory of God.' Whether you are surrendered to God Himself or to a human husband, ultimately it is all submission to God."

Praise God for the counsel of a wise woman, because from that day forward Sandra had a new perspective, and that perspective liberated her. That's not to suggest that it was immediately peaches and cream at home. Her mind, emotions, and will still had to line up with the Word of God time and time again. But the more she placed herself under God's authority, the greater the peace in her home.

> *God doesn't always give you quick answers*
> *when you need to make a decision. So why should you*
> *demand that from your husband?*

Peace, the Gift of God's Love

If submission were a gift box, many of us would be reluctant to open it. We'd be convinced that the contents were oppression and subservience. Yet, in retrospect, my only regret about submission is that it took so long for me to peek inside the gift box, because to my surprise that box was full of peace.

I'd love to be able to invite all the women in the world to spend one day in my home. The spirit of peace abides with us so richly. Did you know that the wife determines the spirit of her home? Yes, the sphere of authority is the husband's, but the sphere of influence belongs to the wife. So powerful is a women's influence that in 1 Corinthians 7:13-14 Paul wrote, "And if a woman has a husband who is not a believer and he is willing to live with her, she must not divorce him. For the unbelieving husband has been sanctified through his wife, and the unbelieving wife has been sanctified through her believing husband. Otherwise your children would be unclean, but as it is, they are holy."

A yielded woman is a force to be reckoned with, and such women are few and far between. In 1 Peter 3:4 we read, "...the unfading beauty of a gentle and quiet spirit...is of great worth in God's sight." What makes something of great worth? Its rarity.

Peace and quiet are by-products of submission. If we're submitted, we've laid all our weapons down. There is no need to defend ourselves because the Lord is our defense. It's unnecessary to fight because "the battle is not ours but the Lord's" (see 2 Chronicles 20:15). It is unprofitable to worry or fret because of what we're told in Philippians 4:6-7: "Do not be anxious about anything, but in everything, by prayer and petition, with thanksgiving, present your requests to God. And the peace of God, which transcends all understanding, will guard your hearts and your minds in Christ Jesus."

One of the most noticeable things about many of the women I've counseled is that they start to look different. They change their makeup; their godly foundation is different. Their hearts are at peace, and that alters their physical appearance. The striving is gone. They stop being on edge and start walking by faith. Laughter returns to their souls, and they become a delight to be around. What a contrast this is to a loud and raging woman who, in her refusal to submit, tears down her house with her own hands. The Bible says such a woman is foolish (Proverbs 14:1).

Submitting with Perseverance

James 1:2 admonishes us, "Consider it pure joy, my brothers, when you face trials of many kinds, because you know that the testing of your faith develops perseverance. Perseverance must finish its work so that you may be mature and complete, not lacking anything."

Submission requires perseverance, but consider the rewards. When God has finished His process, we'll be complete. When I turn on my computer, it begins to load and you can actually watch the numbers climb as it shows the percent of completeness. Once it hits one hundred percent, I am then free to work to my heart's content. My hard drive is running on full capacity. But it takes time to load up.

We live in quick-fix society. We don't like to wait and we don't want to persevere. The definition of persevere is "to persist in a state, enterprise, or undertaking in spite of counter influences, opposition or discouragement." Boy, it takes all of that to appropriate the principle of submission in our lives. There is so much opposition, not only from those who are not believers but, sadly, even from those who *are* Christians. The wry smiles, smug expressions, and discouraging words that enter the scene when I mention the word "submission" tell me all I need to know about some women's hearts.

You don't break God's laws; they break you!

But I've never said that submission is easy. There are long days and nights when we try to do our best and no one seems to notice. Worse yet, those whom we are trying to serve with submission are sometimes downright ungrateful. That's when perseverance kicks in. That's when we know the level of our commitment is to obey God's Word no matter what. And I am happy to announce that God is faithful!

Please don't give up and leave this world without having tasted the wonderful liberation that comes with practicing submission. It will utterly revolutionize your relationships, your home, your family. It may seem at first as if everyone around you is changing in a positive way. In fact, *you're* the one who is becoming new.

Suffice it to say that submission is a powerful, positive, and aggressive principle designed by God for every man and woman, single and married person. A wise person once said, "You don't break God's laws; they break you!" God's law of submission will break the negative patterns in your home, office, and church.

If the word "submission" makes the hair stand up on the back of your neck, you've fallen victim to the wrong definition and application of God's liberating principle. Don't let the world or uninformed Christians restrict you in this area when God has provided freedom. He has chosen to intervene on our behalf when we do things decently and in order. If you have not experienced submission in operation in your own life, then I've got news for you—you've been robbed!

Chapter Three Workbook

Reflection:

Before you understood how the principle of submission worked, what was your response when the word was mentioned?

Do you remember the first time you applied submission *properly* to your life? What happened? If you're yet to experience it, leave this space open until you do.

Meditation:

Scripture Memory:
*"And whatever you do, whether in word or deed,
do it all in the name of the Lord Jesus, giving
thanks to God the Father through him"*
(Colossians 3:17).

Response:

Document your submission journey.

4

Go for the Gold

I am a submitted servant...

In your imagination, I'd like you to travel with me to 1940. Look carefully and you'll see a small-framed woman leaning up against a hospital window in Tennessee, gazing in at the newborn babies in the nursery. The one on the right is hers.

The woman is murmuring, "The doctors say you ain't gonna make it. But they don't know *what* I know, and they don't know *Who* I know."

After awhile, she takes her two-month premature, 4½ pound baby home to the infant's 19 brothers and sisters. But this baby is not like any of the woman's other children. This little girl is always sickly. And even though the home is filled with love, the family lives in poor conditions, with no electricity and no running water. Their bathroom is an outhouse.

As a toddler, the little girl contracts scarlet fever and double pneumonia. But it is polio that cripples her left leg and foot.

As she grows older, the girl watches her brothers and sisters playing in the front yard. Now and then she says, "Momma, I just wanna feel the wind against my face when I run."

Her mother, who worked as a maid, heard that she might find help for her daughter at Maherry Medical School, which is located in a different city. So twice a week, on her days off, the mother and child set off on a three-hour bus trip. The doctors at the clinic say the little girl's prognosis is poor, but if she comes in three times a week for massages and exercises, there is a slim chance that she will get better.

This mother doesn't have the time or money to continue her visits to the clinic, so she asks the professionals to teach her how to do the treatment herself. Every day when she comes home exhausted from cleaning big Southern mansions, she finds her children waiting for her. She knows that only God Himself can strengthen her enough to organize the dinner and help with the children's homework. Then once the other children are in bed, she massages her crippled little girl's leg.

She very possibly sang the old hymn that says, "I don't feel no ways tired. I've come too far from where I started from. Nobody told me the road would be easy; I don't believe He brought me this far to leave me."

For the first year there is no change at all. But slowly the child grows stronger. She stands in one place in the backyard for hours and shoots a basketball at a hoop. One fateful day, when she is eight years old, the little girl wakes up on a Sunday morning, her heart pounding joyfully against her chest.

"Today is the day!" she tells herself.

The little girl has been secretly teaching herself how to walk. When the family arrives at church that morning, she takes off her brace and, to the amazement of the congregation, walks down the church aisle. It isn't until she is 12 years old, however, that the brace officially comes off.

In high school she makes the girls' basketball team, and later a coach from Tennessee A&I gives her a scholarship to run track. In 1960 she stands tall and straight in her place in the Olympics at the Coliseum in Rome. As she bends down at the starting line, she feels as if her mother were right beside her, taking every step and every breath. And, when all is said and done, Wilma Rudolph breaks the tape of the 100-, 200-, and 400-meter races. She becomes the first American woman in history to win three Olympic gold medals. And even though it has been 40 years since those races took place, Wilma's story remains both exciting and inspiring.

As the thunderous roar of applause burst forth from 80,000 spectators in celebration of Wilma's victory, I wonder how many of those attendees knew that her mother's name was Blanche, and that she was her daughter's silent partner. The one who first enabled Wilma to accomplish great things.

"The doctors told me I would never walk again. My mother told me I would. I chose to believe my mother," Wilma said.

Do you think Blanche massaged Wilma's leg daily because she believed her daughter would be an Olympic champion? No, Blanche simply wanted to give Wilma a chance at a healthy existence and was willing to sacrifice some of the best years of her own life to make it happen. She could have rationalized that having 19 healthy children before Wilma was a good ratio and simply accepted her twentieth child's condition. Being invited to the White House with her daughter to be honored by the president was the farthest thing from her mind.

> *"The doctors told me I would never walk again.*
> *My mother told me I would. I chose to believe my mother,"*
> *Wilma said.*

We know that Wilma was not alone when she won that race. Her mother's race was different than her daughter's, but she too had marathon endurance. In fact, according to God's Word, we are all in a race. The Apostle Paul says:

> *Do you not know that those who run in a race all run, but one receives the prize? Run in such a way that you may obtain it. And everyone who competes for the prize is temperate in all things. Now they do it to obtain a perishable crown, but we for an imperishable crown* (1 Corinthians 9:24-25 NKJV).

Our imperishable crown resides in heaven, where we will live and celebrate our victory for all eternity. But first it is necessary that we understand one of God's most basic but profound principles. He wants us to run in a race that challenges us not to *do* but to *be*.

If in your race in life you are frustrated, tired, angry, depressed, despondent, despairing, doubtful, or anguished, it means you're running in the wrong race, headed toward the wrong goal. As we've noted before, God's Word promises, "...but those who hope in the LORD will renew their strength. They will soar on wings like eagles; they will run and not grow weary, they will walk and not faint" (Isaiah 40:31). However, it's essential we're running on the right track.

Getting on the Right Track

The Bible points out we have two possible life tracks on which to run. Both begin with the letter "s." The world's track says "self." Let me see if you can guess what the Lord's track says. What word gives us our best opportunity to *go for the gold*? Before I tell you, I'd like you to fill in these three blanks:

1. Jesus came to demonstrate this principle on earth. He came to _____.

2. If you want to be the greatest among your brothers and sisters in Christ you will be a

   _____.

3. Most Christians use this phrase when you ask them the question, "When you see Jesus what do you want Him to say to you?" " _____."

Here are the answers:

1. Matthew 20:28 tells us that Jesus did not come to be served but to *serve*.

2. Matthew 23:11 says, "The greatest among you will be your *servant*."

3. What do most Christians say they want to hear Jesus state when they see Him face-to-face? "Well done, My good and faithful *servant!*"

The world's track says "self." It runs alongside God's track, which says "servant." And the two tracks run parallel, so it is possible for us to ever-so-slowly veer off from the Lord's plan for our lives and find ourselves running on the "self" track. Being a servant may not be the most appealing idea you've ever heard, but it is God's will for each of us. That's why serving God by serving others is far more rewarding than serving ourselves.

Actually, most of us are very familiar with the principle of servanthood. Let me give you some examples. My husband, Frank, and I celebrated our twenty-fifth wedding anniversary at a five-star hotel—one of the top four hotels in the world.

During our stay, whenever we approached the employees with a question, they didn't say, "How can I help you?" They said, "How may I *serve* you?"

When the employees finished helping us and we thanked them, they replied, "It was my pleasure! Is there anything else I can do to *serve* you?"

Do we think it is strange when we hear hotel employees use the word "serve," or are we impressed? Do you think the hotel staff, from the manager on down, find it demeaning to serve their guests? Or are they instead honored to work for such an illustrious establishment? When I couldn't find my way to a particular location in the hotel, an employee stopped what she was doing and walked with me to my destination. If we even looked like we needed something, the staff seemed to anticipate our every requirement. It was service at its finest.

And that's not only the story at five-star hotels. We see "Outstanding Service Award" plaques on the walls of businesses. And it would not seem strange to hear a pastor recognize one of his congregants by saying, "This woman has been a faithful servant to this church for 40 years." In these circumstances, we rarely find the word "servant" offensive. As a matter of fact, it is often used as a compliment. However, a great deception concerning this principle has been perpetrated against us as women, in particular, and Christian believers as a whole. I think it's time to open our hearts so that God's truth can set us free.

Our Christian Calling

Who is called to be a servant? The call to servanthood includes every Christian, including the single, the single parent, the divorced, the widowed, those married without children, those married with children at home, those married with grown children, and senior citizens. Did I forget anyone? I hope not, but as I move through the rest of this chapter, I want you to think only of yourself. What is God speaking to *you*? When you stand before the judgment seat of Christ to answer for the works you've done on earth, you'll stand alone. So this teaching is for you.

"Self" or "servant." Which track will you run on? In 2 Timothy 3:1-2, God's Word says, "...in the last days... people will be lovers of themselves...." Galatians 5:17 explains, "For the flesh lusteth against the Spirit, and the Spirit against the flesh: and these are contrary the one to the other: so that ye cannot do the things that ye would" (KJV).

If you're a sincere believer, you will agree that you do not want to run on a track called "self." And as I said earlier, the tracks run side by side, so if we're not careful we can be quickly and easily tricked into thinking we're running for Jesus when we aren't. But how do we begin to run the race of servanthood? If "servant" is our track, what is our goal and where are we running?

Our starting block is found in Luke 10:38-42:

> *As Jesus and his disciples were on their way, he came to a village where a woman named Martha opened her home to him. She had a sister called Mary, who sat at the Lord's feet listening to what he said. But Martha was distracted by all the preparations that had to be made. She came to him and asked, "Lord, don't you care that my sister has left me to do the work by myself? Tell her to help me!"*
>
> *"Martha, Martha," the Lord answered, "you are worried and upset about many things, but*

only one thing is needed. Mary has chosen what
is better, and it will not be taken away from her."

The "better" thing Mary chose was to sit at the Lord's feet listening to what He was teaching.

The servant's race begins with *being still* instead of *doing* what we think is right. As we listen and discern the heart of God for our life, He begins to do things through us because He can see that we are yielded vessels. People who run down the track called "self" are in a constant state of doing. They're always trying to fix things, to make something work, to take control, to determine the outcome. They run in anxiety. Those on the track of servanthood run with patience, knowing they have a silent Partner who will enable them to finish the race in victory.

As we sit at the Master's feet listening, one of the first things we learn is that we are not running against another person. Just as in a race, we're running against the clock. In Psalm 139 we read, "All the days ordained for me were written in your book before one of them came to be" (verse 16). That means only God knows the beginning and the ending of your life and mine. Jesus admonishes us to "work while it is day for there comes a time when no man can work" (see John 9:4), and He continues in Revelation 22:12 when He says, "And behold, I come quickly; and my reward is with me, to give every man according as his work shall be" (KJV). Throughout God's Word we are challenged to make the most of our time.

The servant's race begins with being still instead
of doing what we think is right.

As I often teach, the Bible says that "one day with the Lord is like a thousand years on earth" (see 2 Peter 3:8). Did you know that if you broke that equation down, it would mean that by the time we live to be 75 years old, only one hour and 48 minutes would have passed in heaven? I don't know what you're going through in your life, but I have only about 30 minutes left, and I still have a lot of running to do! That makes time the most precious commodity on earth. You can spend money and get it back, but when you spend time it's gone for good.

Doing All to the Glory of God

As we kneel at the starting block, we find the word "servant" written down on the track. A clock hanging to our right started ticking the day we were born, and only God knows when it will stop. As we look down to the end of the course, we see a tape stretched across the finish line. There's something written on it, and I think you should know what it says. Remember when I asked the question, "What is our goal and where are we running?"

Our goal is written on the tape. It says, "For Christ's sake," and it is followed by a Scripture that says, "And whatever you do, whether in word or deed, do it all in the name of the Lord Jesus..." (Colossians 3:17). What is "whatever"? What is "all"? It is *everything*. It is vital that we run for "Christ's sake" because we'll be defeated if we are running for any other reason. If we are looking for our rewards from men or women, Jeremiah 17:5-7 says we are cursed. The Scripture reads:

> *Cursed is the one who trusts in man, who depends*
> *on flesh for his strength and whose heart turns*
> *away from the LORD. He will be like a bush in the*

*wastelands…but blessed is the man who trusts in
the LORD, whose confidence is in him. He will be
like a tree planted by the water.…*

This is why the race begins with sitting at the Lord's feet listening to what He says and ends with, "Whatever you do in word or deed, do it all in the name of the Lord Jesus." And guess what ties those two Scriptures together? It runs along the wall of the bleachers where the people are standing. It says, "Thou shalt love the Lord thy God with all thy heart, mind, soul and strength and thy neighbor as thyself" (see Mark 12:30-31).

And do you know who is standing in the bleachers? Hebrews 12:1-2 says:

*Therefore, since we are surrounded by such a great
cloud of witnesses, let us throw off everything that
hinders and the sin that so easily entangles, and
let us run with perseverance the race marked out
for us. Let us fix our eyes on Jesus, the author and
perfecter of our faith, who for the joy set before
him endured the cross, scorning its shame, and sat
down at the right hand of the throne of God.*

The testimonies of those who have run the race before us are cheering us on, including those of our loved ones who have gone home to glory.

Now that we know the goal is to *be* instead of to *do*, what are we running to? Where is the track heading? I don't know the race that has been marked out for you. For each of us, the answer to that question will be different because we are not in the same season in our lives. Some of us are single, some are married, some are young, and some not so young. One of the worst experiences in life is to attempt to run someone else's race. Therefore, I can tell what's at your finish line, but I don't know the direction your track will take.

I can, however, tell you about my own personal race in order to provide encouragement in yours.

> *The testimonies of those who have run the race before us are cheering us on, including those of our loved ones who have gone home to glory.*

My Own Personal Race

Just like Wilma Rudolph, I too was once crippled. Before I came to know Jesus as my Lord, I had the double pneumonia of rebellion, the scarlet fever of sin, and the polio of independence. God could have looked at all His other healthy children and ignored my condition. But as soon I asked Him to be my Savior, He sent me a silent Partner, the Holy Spirit, to come and live inside of me. Like Wilma's faithful mother, Blanche, this incredible Friend did not grow weary as year after year He massaged away my doubts and fears. Slowly I began to see changes in my life.

For a very long time, I ran on the track called "self." Because I did it in Jesus' name, no one could convince me that I was on the wrong track. I was always doing something, forever busy. Sure, I had devotional times, but they were one-sided. I even got up early in the morning to meet with God, so I was sure I was on the right track.

One morning I went to my prayer closet, which was the bathroom, at 5 A.M. It was the only place in the house where I was assured of privacy. As I knelt by the bathtub and began to pray, the Lord spoke into my heart and posed a very simple question. He asked, "Why are you here?"

I stuttered, "I...I...came to pray."

His response was, "But my Word teaches that you are to pray without ceasing. If you came to pray, what were you doing while you were on the way here?"

Of course, I didn't have an answer for that, so I continued, "Well, I came to give thanks."

God quickly responded, "My Word says to give thanks in all things."

"Okay, I came to rejoice."

"You are to 'rejoice evermore.'"

Having finally reached a point of frustration, I asked, "Okay, so why *am* I here? I could have been sleeping."

The Lord's response was gentle. "You are here to do what you cannot do while you're busy. You are here to *fellowship* with Me."

God continued by showing me an example. He asked, "Suppose you have a friend who calls you regularly. When she finishes talking at length about what's going on in her life, when she's done telling you her troubles, she always says, 'Well, I have to go now.'"

It didn't take long for me to respond, "I would think she was selfish, rude, self-centered, and thoughtless."

The Lord didn't hesitate before He replied, "Have you ever noticed that when you come to pray, you give Me thanks, you rejoice, you tell Me what's on your heart, and then you promptly end with, 'In Jesus' name'? Can't you see that's like hanging up the telephone on Me? Don't you think I have anything to say? Even if I'm silent, don't you think it would be polite to invite Me to share My thoughts with you and then wait and listen to hear My response?"

From that day forward I spent time truly fellowshipping with God. I learned to be still and let Him talk to me. If I thought I heard Him giving me direction about some particular area of my life, I waited for it to be confirmed through His written Word, through the spoken Word, and through the confirmation of two or three witnesses who also fellowshipped with Him. It took me awhile, however, to understand the difference between *being* and *doing*. I believed that *doing* works for the Lord is what He wanted.

So I put on my uniform with "submission" written across the back. I then strapped on the track shoes that said "sacrificial love" and documented the freedom that comes with it in my book *Betrayal's Baby*. I began running in the grass alongside the track that said "servant." I knew Jesus didn't come to be served, but to serve. However, I didn't know how that principle would apply in my own life.

But I finally decided that I wanted to run the race on the real track. I approached and bent down at the starting line. I saw words inscribed across it. The inscription read: "Do nothing out of selfish ambition or vain conceit, but in humility consider others better than yourselves" (Philippians 2:3).

I jumped up and emphatically stated, "Whoa! Wait a minute. I don't mind helping people, but I do have some ambitions of my own. There are things I want to accomplish, and I think they're important."

My silent Partner, the Holy Spirit, gently explained that the Lord had no problem with me having ambitions. He did not, however, want me to have *selfish* ambitions—ambitions that would motivate me to do things out of season and out of order at the expense of others. As a matter of fact, Philippians 2:4 goes on to say, "Each of you should look not only to your own interests, but also to the interests of others."

Once I understood that, I bent down again at the starting line. When the gun sounded, I announced to the Lord I was trusting Him to run through me, to lead me in the direction I should go. That I no longer wanted to *do*, I only wanted to *be* what He called me to be. So where was He taking me? To my surprise, the track was headed home. He was turning my heart toward home.

Going Home

I once heard a pastor say he woke up one winter morning and the sun was so bright, he just knew it was warm outside. Without bothering to put on a coat, he opened the door and discovered it was actually freezing outside. He said he couldn't understand how it could be so bright and sunny and yet so cold. Shortly after that someone told him that in the wintertime, the sun is actually closer to the earth but the rays are pointed in the other direction. In my own life, God helped me see that for many of the years I had been traveling homeward, but like that winter sun, my heart had been pointed in other directions.

So He began teaching me servanthood at home. First I needed to understand the definition of a servant. A servant is someone who anticipates the needs of the person he or she is serving—and then serves without thought of appreciation, thanksgiving, or gratitude. The reward comes from the very act of serving. As I looked at my relationship with my husband, I realized I had done many things for Frank, but I had not served him. I didn't offer him the kind of service that anticipates his needs, that puts his agenda first, that looks for ways to please him without thought of anything in return. So one of the first things I felt led to do was reduce my speaking schedule.

"But," I wondered, "isn't speaking and teaching a good work for the Lord? Aren't people's lives and hearts being changed when I speak? Aren't sinners giving their hearts to Christ?" Once again my silent Partner explained that it was indeed a good work, but based on the season of my life, I didn't have the *time* to do all that speaking. There was a much greater calling on my life for this season, and it would be found in my home serving my husband, children, church, neighborhood, extended family, and others.

It was then that my silent Partner took me back to the illustrations on service. And that's when one of the greatest deceptions perpetrated on married women was revealed.

The Holy Spirit showed me how Mother Teresa has been rightly applauded for serving people she did not know. It was also acceptable to go to an upscale establishment and hear people ask, "How may I serve you?" And how businesses prided themselves on their "Outstanding Service Award." And also how proud we are to be recognized as faithful "servants" in church. But let's say a husband proudly announces, "My wife has been a servant to me for 20 years." In today's world, wouldn't that woman be considered a fool?

It became clear that the world applauds service when it is done to people we don't know, or if we are getting a paycheck for it, or if it is in the church. But it is a disgrace to serve at home. Why? Because the devil knows that it's at home where we reproduce a godly heritage and *we can't reproduce what we don't produce.* Somehow servanthood, one of the most powerful principles found in God's Word, has come to be disdained in our homes.

When I understood the deception, I stood up to the face of the devil and announced, "How dare you tell me who I can serve?" I thought about Paul, who said, "I am a fool for Christ," and I acknowledged that I was willing to be thought of as a fool by the world, as long as I knew that God was being glorified in the process.

I recalled that years before, when I was an administrative assistant to the presidents of various companies, I was outstanding in my service to them. Then and there, I determined that if I didn't accomplish anything else in life, I would serve my husband even better than I had served those men.

> *Let's say a husband proudly announces, "My wife has been a faithful servant to me for 20 years." In today's world, wouldn't that woman be considered a fool?*

And why not serve my husband? Frank is the one person in my life who has promised to be with me for better or for worse, for richer or for poorer, in sickness and in health, until death do us part. I realized how much I wanted our oneness to be a witness to others, and I didn't care whether my husband appreciated my efforts or not. It didn't even matter if I thought he deserved it or not. All I cared about was racing down the "servant" track.

Shortly after I made the commitment to selflessly serve my husband, I discovered my quiet decision was having a profound impact on our home. One day a woman who came to visit me arrived a little earlier than expected. She waited alone for awhile in our living room. When I came downstairs, I found her sitting on the sofa, weeping.

"What's wrong?" I asked, deeply concerned.

She replied, "The spirit of peace is so thick in this house, it caused me to weep. I really needed to be here."

Before long, God showed me another reason He was calling me home. Titus 2:4-5 instructs the older women to "teach the young women to…love their husbands, to love their children, to be…keepers at home…" (KJV). How could I teach women to be "keepers at home" if I wasn't keeping mine? It takes *time* to be a keeper at home.

For years I was a housewife. I lived in a *house* and I was married, which made me a *wife*, and that's why I was a *housewife*. But being a "keeper at home" takes time as you determine what you want your home to be. I want my home to be a haven, a safe harbor for my husband and children. They fight against the world all day, but when they return home they come into a sheltering harbor. And they aren't the only ones who come. Friends, extended family, and strangers visit our home, too.

Think about this—the root word for "hospitality" is "hospital." Paul writes, "Be given to hospitality" (see 1 Timothy 3:2). This means that when people come into my home, they should feel like they are in a hospital being cared for. They should feel better when they leave—mentally, emotionally, and physically. And that takes a plan.

"Decently and in Order"

I realized I was not only called to be a homemaker but also a caretaker. It is my responsibility to take care of what God has so graciously given to me. Luke 16:11-12 says, "So if you have not been trustworthy in handling worldly wealth, who will trust you with true riches? And if you have not been trustworthy with someone else's property, who will give you property of your own?"

As much as I love my home, it will one day belong to another man or woman. When my husband and I go to glory, someone else will own our house. When I keep my home well-maintained and nicely landscaped, its value increases. And not only that, I must also be faithful to my neighbors. The way I take care of my property can directly affect their property value positively or negatively. I want my neighbors to be grateful that I live on their block.

Scripture says, "Let all things be done decently and in order" (1 Corinthians 14:40 KJV). Putting my house in order takes *time*. This goes beyond cleaning or straightening it. That means putting in order the closets, the drawers, underneath my bed. God help me! That also means teaching Gabrielle, who is my only child still at home, to be orderly by helping her organize her own room.

For years I nagged my other children about cleaning up their rooms, which they did very reluctantly. Their rooms only stayed neat for one day because I had never helped them organize so they could experience living decently and in order. Then I discovered a book that every woman, single or married, needs to buy—*More Hours in My Day* by Emilie Barnes. You know how I used to clean? I'd put a trashcan at the end of a counter and with one swoop, the mess would be wiped away. I owned 10 pairs of scissors because I couldn't find one. Emilie Barnes' book changed my life.

I've also discovered that it takes *time* to put things in order for emergencies. We live in California. If an earthquake were to hit right now and there was structural damage to our home, my family would be able to live in the yard for up to two weeks without any outside assistance. We have sufficient water, food, tents, and sleeping bags, and we're equipped for sanitation needs and medical emergencies. All that preparation took *time*.

It also took *time* to put our papers in order concerning our wills, to make sure that what God has given us is not eaten up in probate taxes. When Frank and I go to see the Lord, everything will be done decently and in order for our family.

And it takes *time* and a spirit of servanthood to be a witness to our neighbors. One day not long ago, while I was taking my daily walk up and down my block, I was stopped by one of my neighbors. She wanted to know if I had heard about another neighbor's illness. She had brain cancer. This woman had a husband and two teenage sons, and I knew she needed help. I prepared a full-course dinner and dropped it off at the house. And that took *time*.

A couple of days later as I was about to put a note on the woman's door letting her know I was available to do anything for her—drive her to doctor's appointments, help out in any way—she opened the door. She invited me in, and we walked together to the kitchen. I noticed it wasn't clean and understood how difficult it would be for her to clean it, considering her illness. As she talked, I began to clean. It took about an hour, and as I finished mopping the floor, she asked me to sit down.

"You know I'm a Muslim," she said.

I told her I knew that. As we continued, I asked her, "Who do you say Jesus is?"

Her reply was, "He was a messenger."

I nodded and asked, "What was His message?"

Of course, she believed that He was a messenger of love and peace.

"Did you know," I continued, "that in the Bible, Jesus said He didn't come to bring peace but a sword? That He has the 'keys to death, hell, and the grave' and that He is 'the way, the truth, and the life.' No man comes to the father but by Him?"

For the next half hour the Lord provided an opportunity for me to share with this woman the gift of salvation. I don't know if she received it, but I rejoiced in my heart that it had been offered. Do you know what that took? It took *time*.

I then understood the parable Jesus taught of the 100 sheep. One had gotten lost and the question was, "Who will leave the 99 sheep (the job, the ministry, the career) to go find the one?" That one sheep may be a husband, a child, a neighbor, a convict, a senior citizen, or someone else. Who will take the *time*?

I hope your answer—like mine—is, "I will."

Humble Yourself, and He Will Lift You Up

One of the most amazing aspects of service is that the more we lift others up, the more the Lord does things for us. And frequently the things He does for us often don't require us to invest our time. Here's an example. It has long been my heart's desire that men and women be set free with the message of submission.

One day, while I was intent on serving my husband, I got a call from a radio ministry that has over 500 syndicated stations across the United States. Someone had sent the station a tape of my message on submission, which I had delivered at the Rose Bowl stadium in 1997. The station executives wanted to air it in its entirety, to be heard by thousands—if not millions—of people. All this, and I never had to leave my home! Better yet, the message received such an overwhelming response that the station aired it four more times, which was very unusual for that ministry.

Since then, my radio interviews have tripled, which means I can stop for half an hour, speak to thousands of people, and then go back to serving my family. It has become clear that while I'm taking care of God's business, He is taking care of mine. God is faithful.

If You're a Married Woman

Now, if you are a married women reading this chapter, perhaps what I have shared has raised questions in your heart. Let me address a few. Like I said at the beginning, I can't speak for where God's track is taking you. He will have to show you. For many of you, it will be the same as mine—the track leads home.

You may be thinking, "Oh, brother! I'm out of here, Bunny. You don't know my husband!"

No, I don't know him. But I know something about him. We live in a free society where we get to choose whom we marry. I hope that no one held a gun to your head when you married your husband. And even if you got married for the wrong reasons, you had a choice as to whom you would marry. Out of all the men you'd ever met, you chose him, which tells me that at one time in your life, you saw qualities in this man that stimulated your decision to dedicate your whole life to him. I know if he is your husband, he stood before a preacher or a justice of the peace and promised to stay with you "until death do us part." This much I know about your husband.

I was doing a live radio talk show one day when a woman called in and said, "What if you married a fool?"

"Well, the first thing you need to do," I responded, "is take responsibility for marrying a fool and then trust God to fix it."

> *You may be thinking, "Oh, brother! I'm out of here, Bunny. You don't know my husband!"*

I went on to point out to her that in the thirteenth chapter of 1 Corinthians we read, "Love suffers long and is kind" (NKJV). The passage goes on to say, "[Love] bears all things, believes all things, hopes all things, endures all things. Love never fails."

"So let me encourage you to be faithful," I concluded, "and allow God to fix anything that appears to be broken. Remember, there is no way to judge the condition of your marriage until you do it God's way."

If you're married, servanthood begins with your husband, because God has honored and sanctified the relationship.

"But, Bunny, he doesn't deserve it!" you may feel like screaming. Well, that's true. None of us deserves having Jesus serve us or having Him die on the cross to purchase our eternal life. As we serve our husbands, our appreciation for the price Christ paid for us grows deeper and deeper every day. It's imperative that we are serving Christ *through* our husbands. Just how would you treat Christ if He came to your home? Transfer that answer to your husband.

But what if your husband doesn't appreciate your efforts? God heard your question before the beginning of time because 1 Peter 2:20 says, "For what credit is it if, when you are beaten for your faults, you take it patiently? But when you do good and suffer, if you take it patiently, this is commendable before God" (NKJV).

The problem is that sometimes the things we do aren't really done for Jesus' sake. They're done for other reasons, selfish ones. Serve Christ through your husband, and God will give you untold joy, even in the midst of your husband's lack of appreciation. At the same time, God will be changing your husband's heart. He's at work in your situation, even if you can't see it with the natural eye.

If You're a Single Parent

Perhaps your track in life involves serving the needs of your children, and because you are single, you are facing the task of serving them without the help of a spouse. One of the most difficult challenges of single parenting is the feeling that everything is up to you. Please let me encourage you to remember that you can't be both father and mother to your children. God did not equip you for that. If you're the mom, you are the nurturer. Let God be the Father to your children.

You can stop screaming at the top of your lungs, trying to get your children to do things. Be clear in your instructions, consistent in your responses, and let them know that when they get out of hand, you are going to talk to their Father. Leave them and go to your prayer closet, which might be your bedroom, bathroom, or another private room. Lift them up to God and watch how He intervenes. It will begin to put the fear of God in their hearts when they realize they are no longer contending with you. They are dealing directly with God, who loves them very much but also believes in firm discipline.

And here's a word to the wise—make sure your children's natural father pays child support. Stop trying to make it easy on him. You send a message of irresponsibility to your children when you don't hold their earthly father accountable for his actions. After all, he was your equal partner in bringing them into the world.

And if you feel weary, remember this: Your children will grow up, and God will lead you to other vistas. Be patient and faithful, and God will honor you.

If You Are Single

If you are single without children, the Apostle Paul says you are in the best position to be totally available to God. You are free to serve anyone and everyone, according to His direction. It is so important for you *to be* instead of *to do* what you think is the most productive. I have a single personal assistant who took a year off her job to come and work for me at no charge. You can only do that kind of thing if you're single.

God can use you to strengthen marriages by offering your services to a married female friend, perhaps watching her children one day of the week at no charge. Or maybe you could cook a complete meal and drop it off so she has time to relax. Or what about reaching out to a single parent who is carrying a tremendous load? Why not chip in and help her? There are convalescent homes to visit, teenagers to mentor, schools that need volunteers. The list of options is endless. This is a season in which God is able to send you out and use you at will.

As I wrote in my book *Knight in Shining Armor*, there is so much preparation for you to do in order to become ready for marriage. Servanthood should begin in your single life and extend over into your marriage. There is also another relevant book available entitled *Secrets of an Irresistible Woman*, written by Michelle McKinney Hammond. She wrote it in response to the popular book *The Rules*. It will bless you.

If You Are a Divorcee, Widow, or Senior Citizen

If you've lost your partner to death or divorce, this season may feel like wintertime to you. You feel cold inside, still aching from the pain of your loss. Let God heal your heart today so you can serve Him and others after this difficult season has passed. There are many hurting people, but you can only help them if you're a whole person. Let God make you whole and then run the "servant" track as He shows you where you're needed.

And you, my senior sisters, have so much to give. You have acquired wisdom over the years, and it's time for you to give that wisdom back in service, whether to grandchildren, grade schools, hospitals, nursing homes, your neighborhood, or your church. It's hard to be depressed when we are thinking about others.

As you age, you may be in pain, but even so God can use you to demonstrate the unexplainable peace that comes when your mind is stayed on Him. And don't get distracted! You don't have time to go to Las Vegas and gamble your latter years away. The senior years are the time for you to become 100-percent dedicated to what God has called you to be.

"Tired In but Not Tired Of"

What track are you running on—"self" or "servant"? What do you want to hear Jesus say when you see Him face-to-face? If it is to be, "Well done, my good and faithful *servant*," then the question is, "Whom are you serving?" I encourage you not to leave this chapter without reflecting on your life and identifying whether you have been running on the "self" track or the "servant" track. If you have been running on the "self" track, it takes a repentant heart to begin anew. Do you know what repentance signifies? It means, "I'm changing."

It would be wonderful if I could tell you that the race is always easy, but it is not. So many times my flesh has cried out to be satisfied by going in another direction. There are times I feel unappreciated and tired. I wish I could tell you that you'll always do it right, but you won't.

Did you know that in the Greek translation of the Bible, the words "servant" and "minister" are the same? When we minister to someone's needs, as Blanche ministered to her daughter Wilma, we are serving that person. And as we serve and minister, it helps tremendously to remember the price Jesus paid to minister to us. When we remember Him, we become strengthened again to run another mile. And it's during those focused times that we experience the incredible peace of God, His "unexplainable peace that passes all understanding." As my pastor says of his own Christian journey, "Sometimes I get tired *in* it, but I never get tired *of* it."

I encourage you to get on the right track. Join me in the race. Let's run together. Let's go for the gold!

Chapter Four Workbook

Reflection:

Which track have you been running on? What has been the result?

Meditation:

Scripture Memory:
"Do nothing out of selfish ambition and vain conceit, but in humility consider others better than yourselves. Each of you should look not only to your own interests, but also to the interests of others"
(Philippians 2:3-4).

Response:

Document your first week of true servanthood.

5

Seasons

I acknowledge the wisdom of identifying and
operating according to my seasons...

When fall takes its final bow and winter rushes in almost immediately afterward, I always grieve the passing of my rose garden. A chill demands that the bushes be cut back, with no trace of their former beauty left behind. After summer has unveiled its hidden splendor, I am equally sorrowful to see it go. However, shortly after the demise of the roses, I notice the azaleas bursting forth in a red-and-pink array. Alongside of them bloom colorful camellias, while birds of paradise proudly display their tropical orange hue. Sad as I feel about the roses, I realize that even in winter, God has no shortage of beauty in His storehouse.

Surely you recognize that I'm describing a Southern California winter. But even in the coldest of temperatures, God adds His beautifying touch to every season. Looking out over a field of freshly fallen snow, gazing at the myriad shapes taken by icicles hanging from a roof, or watching geese fly in formation—these things take our breath away and affirm the glory of God's indescribable creation. And at the end of a winter's day, sitting by a blazing fireplace with hot chocolate in hand is both invigorating and comforting. All kinds of pleasures can also be found in spring, fall, and summer. And the same is true of the seasons in our lives.

The Bible reminds us that to everything there is a season (Ecclesiastes 3:1). We don't measure our life's seasons with changing temperatures, but with changing commitments, and with our location on our spiritual journey. Are you single, a single parent, separated from your spouse, a divorcee or a widow, or married with or without children? With every season we discover different opportunities and challenges. For example, summer brings welcome warmth and leisurely vacations; it also brings flies and mosquitoes. And once we identify our life's season, we can enjoy it and take advantage of its opportunities. And there's one certain and reassuring thing about any season—it won't last forever.

I have recently completed my first yearlong mentoring stint with a fellowship of women, each of whom has been married for less than five years. This monthly gathering of eight women in my home found me teaching them how to cook, with an incorporated Bible study centered around loving their husbands and children and being keepers of the home. One of my main focuses has been to instruct them to live their lives according to their seasons.

When we first began, those who had chosen to stay home and raise their children expressed feelings of frustration as they struggled to balance their time between husband and children while their personal goals and visions were not being addressed. Meanwhile, those who worked outside the home were weary because they wanted to stay home and devote themselves to their children. One homeschooling mother was disturbed by well-meaning friends who constantly questioned her judgment. She had decided to teach her children herself, and had walked away from a lucrative career to do so.

Watching each woman settle into her season was so gratifying. It was a pleasure to see each one learn to enjoy her God-appointed present while slowly and methodically preparing for future change. The Apostle Paul put it so aptly when he said, "for I have learned to be content in whatever circumstances I am" (see Philippians 4:12).

If we are not careful, we'll come to the end of our lives and we'll have missed all the precious present moments. They will have escaped like fluttering birds with no destination. Our memories will consist of pictures caught on film, with all the laughter and joy of the moment blurring into an unclear portrait of the past.

When Gabrielle awakens each morning and comes downstairs, I stop what I'm doing just to hold her. I relish in the opportunity to have one more chance to draw her close. I love to feel the beating of her little heart and smell the sweetness of her skin. I whisper in my daughter's ear, "Gabrielle, the sun came up today. Do you know what that means?"

She answers, "God is faithful."

I respond, "And He'll be faithful to you. No matter how gloomy it gets in your life, always remember the sun is shining behind the clouds, and if you'll be still, the clouds will roll away." Then I pray aloud for her day. It's a little thing and probably has very little meaning to her right now, but it's something I believe she'll hold dear when she's older. And it will be no surprise to see her repeat that precious moment when she has children of her own.

> *I whisper in my daughter's ear, "Gabrielle,*
> *the sun came up today. Do you know what that means?"*
> *She answers, "God is faithful."*

That is the kind of message I tried to impart to the women in my mentoring fellowship. I wanted them to remember that every day, their actions are investments into future generations. Jobs and money come and go, but memories are forever. A woman's down payment into the well-being of her husband and children will pay dividends for all eternity.

A Single Season

In my book *Knight in Shining Armor*, single Christian women and men are challenged to commit six months to dating only the Lord. I ask them to allow Him to prepare them mentally, emotionally, financially, and spiritually for their future spouse (if it is God's desire for them to marry). Letters pour in daily in response to that book, and my travels around the country speaking to singles' groups allows me to listen to the hearts of my readers. Unless single believers have accepted the challenge to commit to quality time with the Lord, there is one word to describe their general state of mind: *anxious*. These people live perpetually in the future, wondering every morning if *this* is the day their lives will change, if *this* is the day they will meet Mr. or Miss Right.

In October 1998, Frank and I met with a leadership group at a Christian resort. The beautiful establishment was nestled between the San Bernardino mountains and was isolated from the world. The woman in charge of the facility (we'll call her Karen) had read my book and had completed her six-month commitment to the Lord. During one of the breaks, she and I had the opportunity to converse. Her desire was to be married, and she had been patiently waiting. I admired how she had been successfully living her single life, but I could tell that concern was beginning to build up inside her. After all, what were her chances of being "found" in such a secluded location?

I told Karen with a smile that while the Lord was looking at her, He was simultaneously looking at her spouse, and He would allow their paths to cross. She seemed to relax. Sure enough, four weeks later a businessman came to their hotel from the East Coast. Within six months he and Karen were married and she was redecorating their brownstone home in New York City.

Now she is a married woman. And if God has His way, that will be her status until "death do them part." Her season of singleness is over. Fortunately, she had many days, weeks, and months of living contentedly in her single life. Cherished memories of personal fulfillment have followed her into marriage. And there are times when she reflects on how blessed she was to have had that solitude with the Lord. Now she struggles to find a daily balance between responding to the needs of her husband, taking care of the family business, and spending quality time with the Lord.

Singleness is a season which is often missed completely. Feelings of loneliness and dissatisfaction get in the way of the intimate fellowship God desires with every single person. He wants us to fellowship with Him without interruption, and the ability to control one's schedule and resources is found far more easily when we are single than when we are married. Unfortunately, the flesh, the world, and the devil consume that precious time. They drive single people to

focus outside of their current state and to anxiously anticipate the time when it will finally change.

Lessons from a Chair

*Why in the world did you plop all your weight down on
that chair without giving it a second thought?*

If you are married, you can relax; if it's your desire to be
married, then you can still relax. Are you sitting in a chair
while reading this book? If not, take time to remember the
last chair you sat in. Hopefully from this day forward, a chair
is going to have great significance to you.

The last time you rested all your weight in a chair, did
you know the person who made the chair? Did you know
where it was manufactured? Did you know the quality of
materials that were used to make it? Then why in the world
did you plop all your weight down on that chair without
giving it a second thought?

It is probably because you made an assumption concerning its safety and good quality. *There is just something
about the nature of a chair that suggests it has been designed to
hold us.* We trust chairs. Even if some chair in the past has
broken under us, we still trust chairs.

God's promises are like that chair. Listen to some of
them:

> *"For I know the plans I have for you," declares the
> LORD, "plans to prosper you and not to harm you,
> plans to give you hope and a future" (Jeremiah
> 29:11).*

Let us not become weary in doing good, for at the proper time, we will reap a harvest if we do not give up (Galatians 6:9 emphasis added).

Be strong and courageous. Do not be terrified; do not be discouraged, for the LORD your God will be with you wherever you go (Joshua 1:9).

Think about this: Are you willing to stand before Christ one day and hear Him tell you that you had more faith in a chair than you had in Him? That you had more *hope* in a chair than you had in Him? I pray that from this day forward, no matter what you are facing in life, a chair will be your constant reminder of the promises of God and a reminder that His Word says He cannot lie. We must grasp that "faith is being sure of what we *hope* for and certain of what we do not see" (Hebrews 11:1 emphasis added).

Here's another way to look at it. If it's God's desire for you to be married, every time you sit down in a chair, you are sitting on the promise that God will provide you with a spouse. He or she is there; God just wants to surprise you with the reality. Throw away your timeline about when you think it should happen. Be content to *know* it will happen and that you have a lot of work to do before your future spouse arrives. Once he or she gets here, you won't have the time to do a lot of things you have time to do now. Your time alone is a privilege.

If God has called you *not* to be married, be assured that your life will be as rich—if not richer—than that of any married person. When He chooses that you should remain single, you belong totally to Him. The Apostle Paul says it is a preferred option because:

An unmarried woman or virgin is concerned about the Lord's affairs: Her aim is to be devoted to the Lord in both body and spirit. But a married woman is concerned about the affairs of this world—how she can please her husband (1 Corinthians 7:34).

Of course, our trust in God covers far more than the question of whether or not we will get married. It can concern a new job or a potential ministry. It can concern how to pay off our bills or how to get control of our eating or spending habits. Whatever affects us in our lives, that chair symbolizes God's desire for us to "cast all our cares [our weight] upon Him because He cares for us" (1 Peter 5:7).

If you are married and struggling with marital challenges, have faith that God is fixing whatever is broken. You have probably read, "Being confident of this very thing that He who has begun a good work in *me* shall complete it until the day of Jesus Christ." Do you believe it? Well, then, replace the word "me" with your husband's or your child's name. He will complete His good work in us *and* in them. Once again, you can relax by faith. You don't have to blow out candles and make a wish, find a four-leaf clover, or go to a psychic to have your fortune read. Your future has already been told, and it's good.

From now on, each time you sit down in a chair, you should smile. Every chair you see should encourage your heart to *know* that God's faithfulness is greater than any piece of furniture you will sit upon. You can trust Him, and you can rest in Him.

Surprise!

On the Fourth of July, my family sometimes attends a local fireworks display. Thousands of people gather at this location in the late afternoon and spread out their blankets in the grass. Some of them play patriotic songs on their tape recorders. As the sky grows darker and darker, we sit with much anticipation and stare into the open black sky. When the first fireworks explode into a burst of colors and designs, oohs and aahs can be heard all around. Now let me ask you a question. How long do you think we would sit there and stare into that black sky if we weren't assured of a colorful and exciting display? Not long.

And even if we do expect a great exhibition, we sometimes become impatient. We keep checking our watches. Even though the wait is well-rewarded at the end, we don't like it a bit when we're in the midst of it. We want to know what is coming next, and we want to know when it's going to get here.

The same is true in our spiritual lives. Too many of us want to *see* what God is going to do next while He wants to throw a surprise party! When I come home from a trip with a gift for Gabrielle, I don't just walk up and give it to her. That would be no fun. I usually hide it behind my back, asking her to close her eyes and waiting for her expression of pure delight when she opens it and discovers what I have selected for her. My joy comes from her happiness, and her happiness comes from the unexpected surprise.

God loves throwing surprise parties, but we always seem to want to have a say about the party plans. We desire to know when, what, and where everything is going to happen to us. But that's no fun. Scripture teaches, "...hope that is seen is no hope at all. Who hopes for what he already has?

But if we wait for what we do not yet have, we wait for it patiently" (Romans 8:24-25).

Let's picture our future as that black sky and stare into it, knowing it will light up in God's timing and that His display of color and light and sound will be beautiful.

When we go to a fireworks display, we usually can't see where the fireworks are set up. Sometimes we can't even see the fireworks go up into the sky. There is no evidence of their existence until they explode in all their dazzling glory. In a similar sense, as I walk through my day I look for God's fireworks displays. As situations unfold, I often smile and exclaim, "Surprise!" as God once again reveals Himself in so many wonderful ways. He delights in the *oohs!* and *aahs!* of His children.

The Married Season

Singles are always waiting for the fireworks, and married women are always wondering why the fireworks ended so quickly. I'm sorry to report that I have met very few happily married women. Most wives spend their time trying to *fix* their husbands and are plagued with an attitude of ingratitude. By the way, many of these unhappy souls are the same women who couldn't wait to get married. We married women need to rest in our season and appreciate every little blessing we are able to enjoy during this time.

"What little blessings, Bunny?" you say. "I'm having a hard time figuring out what little blessings you're talking about."

Well, here's one. Are you grateful for the social covering that comes with marriage? I know that I am. When I walk into a room full of men and women, I can freely meet and greet those in attendance. That's not the case with a single woman. She needs to be fully conscious of how she addresses a single man, not to mention those husbands who may be present. She is under rigid scrutiny as to how she conducts herself. But I'm married to Frank. A single man does not have to wonder whether I'm trying to get him to the altar, and the married men and women know I'm already taken. I love my social covering.

Here's another. What about the physical covering your marriage provides? You may not have the happiest marriage in town. But the very fact that a man is present in your home provides an additional physical security in your life. You are less vulnerable to outside threats and dangers.

Those are just two assets of being married. There are many more. Have you ever made a marriage gratitude list? Our lives are improved when we walk in an attitude of thanksgiving. And you will be pleasantly surprised by the results when you openly share your thoughts of appreciation with your husband. One of the first pleasures arrives when you see God's Word come true in your life. Remember the Scripture, "A man reaps what he sows" (Galatians 6:7)? I used to think I could sow complaints, nagging, and ingratitude in my marriage and reap love and romance. That's not true. We have to plant good seeds in order to reap a good and bountiful harvest.

I suggest that you make a gratitude list and express it every day. Then spend the rest of your life focused on being the best person you can be and taking your eyes off the shortcomings of your spouse. The Bible is very specific in Ephesians 4:29-32:

> *Do not let any unwholesome talk come out of*
> *your mouths, but only what is helpful for building*
> *others up according to their needs, that it may*

*benefit those who listen. And do not grieve the
Holy Spirit of God, with whom you were sealed
for the day of redemption. Get rid of all bitterness,
rage and anger, brawling and slander, along with
every form of malice. Be kind and compassionate
to one another, forgiving each other, just as in
Christ God forgave you.*

Oh, if only we would live according to the Word of God! If every Christian practiced Ephesians 4:29-32, what kind of world would this be? What would be the state of our marriages? It is a fact that everyone wants love, acceptance, and approval, and the Scriptures provide the wisdom we need to have those things. But alas, so many people do not obey God's Word, then place the blame on everything but themselves.

The Loss of a Lifetime

Not long ago, I found myself sitting next to a pastor's wife at a luncheon where I had been invited to speak. I admired the woman's calm demeanor, and her youthful looks defied her age. Some of her daughters, daughters-in-law, and grandchildren were also at our table. You could easily see that they had been influenced by her gracious spirit. This woman had been married over 50 years, and when someone described her relationship with her husband, she said, "That couple is joined at the hip. They are best friends."

Only two months after our meeting, I learned that this pastor's wife is now a pastor's widow. Her husband died suddenly and unexpectedly after baptizing some people at a Saturday night church service. He was instantly taken from earth to Glory. There were no warning signs, and his wife was not present when the Lord called this godly man home. Her grief must have been immeasurable.

How can we begin to fill the emptiness that remains when a spouse dies? What makes it possible for us to face the unoccupied space in our bed or the empty chair at the kitchen table? How do we address the anger in our hearts, the reality that God never asked for our permission to take away the love of our life?

My husband, Frank, is my closest confidant. Many of the thoughts I have and the decisions I make are first discussed with him. What would I do with the loss of someone like that? If the faithfulness of God is seen anywhere on earth, I believe it is most powerfully revealed in the lives of widows and widowers who allow the Lord to fill the void in their life, who invite God to continue to use them in an effective way. These courageous men and women are marching forward under the Lord's banner which reads, "God is faithful."

I've noticed that many widows and widowers don't realize the season they are in and the powerful way in which God uses them in their widowhood. People watch widowed believers closely, especially if the tremendous love the couple had for one another was apparent to all. As onlookers see them going through the grieving process and into the season of restoration, their faith and hope in the living God are stimulated. If a person can suffer such a great loss and recover, then surely our heavenly Father will see us through our own difficult challenges.

Widowhood is a season that is many times overlooked. I pray that organizations within the church will continue to be formed to nurture and develop this wonderful group of hurting and healing people. They are a reservoir of faith and wisdom. Their channeled strength could be a powerful blessing to the entire church fellowship.

If being a widow or widower is your season right now, let me encourage you to allow the Lord to use you in your station in life to bring Him great glory. You are a precious and valuable asset. God wants to wipe away your tears and lift you up.

Expecting the Unexpected

Sometimes we have the luxury of preparing for our next season. When one of my daughters left for college, I knew what was coming and did my best to brace myself for the loss. I was doing quite well until I walked into her bedroom a few days before she left. She was packing her bags. I stood in the doorway and tears began to pour down my face. I knew the pain was coming, but it still hit me broadside. Fortunately, the positive adjustment came along soon enough and I began to enjoy my new season of freedom.

There are seasonal changes, however, which come upon us and catch us totally unawares. We have no time to prepare. We never see them coming. If we are not willing to make quick adjustments, unexpected change can plunge us into a pit of despair.

When Jance and Yvette were married in 1991, he was 40 and she was 34. I had led Yvette to the Lord in her early twenties, and she had continued to love and serve Him from that time on. However, as she entered her thirties, her singleness began to cause her grief. She wanted so much to be married and have children. Finally Jance, her "knight in shining armor," arrived. You should have seen Yvette in her wedding dress! Tall, thin, and stately, she walked down the aisle like a queen, and we all cried.

In October 1994, Yvette gave birth to Mary Paige. When the time for delivery came, a nurse told Yvette not to push when she felt the baby coming, but instead to wait for her doctor to arrive. He showed up 45 minutes later. Needless to say, Yvette was in considerable discomfort and distress.

When the baby was born, she weighed only 5 pounds, 8 ounces. And Yvette noticed something was wrong right away. Mary Paige would not nurse. Yvette was so determined to give her daughter breast milk that she pumped it into a bottle. The infant was 18 weeks old before she nursed for the first time. She didn't crawl until she reached eight months. She didn't walk until she was over a year and a half old.

When Mary Paige was three, Yvette and Jance took her to a number of doctors who put her through a battery of tests. Her diagnoses included everything from autism to mild retardation. The medical experts agreed that the child would need to be put in special classes and that the parents would have to learn to live with their daughter's limitations.

But Yvette didn't believe the experts. She could see intelligence in her child's eyes, and no one could convince her otherwise. One day she picked up a book entitled *How to Teach Your Baby to Read*. The book's author, Glenn Donan, included directions for teaching a brain-injured child to read. Reading the book, Yvette instantly knew that Mary Paige had an undiagnosed brain injury.

She called the Institute for the Development of Human Potential and signed up for their next class in Philadelphia. During that weeklong course, the institute taught parents how to heal their brain-injured children. Since then, Yvette has taken Mary Paige out of school and now spends five hours a day going through various exercises and activities. This rigorous, highly disciplined, and exhaustive program can take from six months to two years to achieve results. Every single day, as Yvette works with Mary Paige, she reminds herself that her efforts are only for a season.

When Yvette took on this task of teaching her child, she was also working to develop a rapidly growing company. Everything in her life came to a halt except her commitment to seeing Mary Paige whole and healthy. She was willing to pay the price, and I look forward to watching her reap the rewards. Yvette has learned to live in her season and to wait for another time to pursue her other interests. She is living in the present, making the most of "now."

The Season of "Now"

"Now" is the only time we have. We can't reclaim the past, and we cannot see into the future. All we have is this day, this hour, this minute, this second. What will you do with your "now"? Are you breathing? Be grateful. Can you see well enough to read the words in this book? Be thankful. But don't just acknowledge the good things in your life. Rejoice in them, thank God for them every day, all day. Your life, your attitude, and your actions will fall into line behind gratitude, and your world will begin to change for the better.

One of the most unhappy places we can choose to live is in a state of "If only..." We dream and imagine and create a fantasy about something that we don't have, something someone hasn't done, or something we think we can't live without. What does this kind of thinking do? It makes us ungrateful, unhappy, and unwilling to meet the challenges we face. It makes us unable to rejoice in all the things we have *now*. Singles often say, "I'd be happy *if only* I were married." But singles aren't the only ones who allow *if only* thinking to ruin their present season. It's a bad habit that can erode the blessings of any season of our lives. Let's thank God for what we *do* have instead of worrying constantly about what we *don't* have.

What season are you in right now? Ask God to help you see what this particular season requires of you and how you can best live within the "now" of it while bearing the spiritual fruits of faith, hope, and love. One of these days, the roses in my garden are going to bud and bloom again; it's inevitable. And one of these days, your dreams are going to put forth shoots of new life and buds of promise. They will have survived enough seasons to be recognized as your lifelong desires. And, as you delight yourself in Him, God will give you the desires of your heart.

*Let's thank God for what we **do** have instead of worrying constantly about what we **don't** have.*

Chapter Five Workbook

Reflection:

What season are you experiencing in your life right now? How have you been responding? If you are not responding well, what decisions will you make from this day foward to change that?

Meditation:

Scripture Memory:
"To every thing there is a season…"
(Ecclesiastes 3:11 KJV).

"'For I know the plans I have for you,' declares the LORD, 'plans to prosper you and not to harm you, plans to give you hope and a future'"
(Jeremiah 29:11).

Response:

Write a gratitude list. Post it where you can see it and read it every day.

6

Follow the Yellow Brick Road

I recognize that my success comes from the Lord...

I often hear my husband quote, "Most of us spend our lives climbing the ladder of success only to discover that when we get to the top, it is leaning up against the wrong building!" That's an amusing word picture, one which requires us to ask ourselves a very important question: What is genuine success? For one thing, success is the progressive realization of worthwhile goals. Many Christians would agree that for them, success means living the abundant life promised by Jesus when He said, "I am come that they might have life, and that they might have it more abundantly" (John 10:10b KJV). For believers, a successful existence is one that is full of God's peace, contentment, fulfillment, and purpose.

In the fictional story *The Wizard of Oz*, Dorothy travels a road to success and uncovers some obstacles along the way to her destination. Dorothy's goal was to find the Wizard so she could return home. She followed the Yellow Brick Road and faced many challenges. And along the way she met three unique characters—a Lion who had no courage, the

Scarecrow who, in addition to having no brain, had very little spine, and the Tin Man who had no heart. These characters can illustrate for us that fear, a lack of endurance, and a crippled emotional life can sabotage our chances of reaching our potential.

For the love of her family, Dorothy eventually found her way back home. For the love of the Lord, we are also assured of finding our way to success and fulfillment. Yes, there will be obstacles, but we are promised in Proverbs 21:21, "He who pursues righteousness and love finds life, prosperity and honor." But it's necessary that we place our trust in God. Proverbs 3:5-6 advises us to "trust in the LORD with *all* your heart and lean not on your own understanding; in all your ways acknowledge him, and *he will make your paths straight.*"

Dorothy's fable reminds us to keep moving. And Dorothy constantly found herself in situations that caused her to wonder if she was going the wrong way. She kept moving forward anyway.

If we were to spiritualize Dorothy's journey, Glinda, the good witch, would represent Wisdom, which we learned about in chapter 2. At each crossroads, Dorothy received direction. Her dog, Toto, always by her side, represents the constant presence of God and His faithfulness. John 16:13 states, "But when he, the Spirit of truth comes, he will guide you into all truth." It is so comforting to know that we are not alone.

> *The devil doesn't know everything, but he does seem to be aware of how God has specifically gifted each of us. And it's in the areas of our best gifts that he launches his strongest attacks.*

The Fearful Lion

When Dorothy met the Lion, he tried to scare her with his size, but she refused to be intimidated. When she said, "Boo!" the terrified animal ran and hid, paralyzed by his own fear. I once heard the acronym for F.E.A.R. is "false evidence appearing real." Of course, some fears warn us of real danger, but most of the fears we face are far less threatening than they appear to be. Fear itself, nonetheless, is a great obstacle for everyone. Fear stops us from moving forward in our life. Like the Lion, our various fears paralyze us—fear of failure, fear of success, fear of rejection, fear of shame, and perhaps worst of all, fear of fear.

While we are young, our archenemy, Satan, spends a lot of time planting seeds of fear in our hearts to hinder our growth, both present and future. Thanks to him, we feel somehow inadequate. Every effort, every new venture, is too scary, and we become more and more satisfied in simply existing. When fear has us that immobilized, just making it through a day qualifies as a success. The devil doesn't know everything, but he does seem to be aware of how God has specifically gifted each of us. And it's in the areas of our best gifts that he launches his strongest attacks.

On my daily walks I pass a large black dog who lives behind a concrete wall. He barks ferociously through a wrought-iron gate whenever I walk by. The first few times I heard him, I nearly jumped out of my skin. Then I began speaking to the dog as I passed. That seemed to upset him even more. One day I decided to walk up to the gate. I stopped and looked directly into the dog's eyes as I spoke. Do you know what he did? He ran under a bush and shivered like a frightened puppy.

Many of our fears are like that loud, black dog. Once we walk toward them, they either disappear or become so small that it seems hard to believe they ever intimidated us.

When I married Frank, we lived in a house on a hill with a panoramic view. There were large sliding glass doors in every room, stretching across the whole house, and open-weave shades were our window dressing. Even when they were closed we could still see the lights of the city. I was fairly sure that if I could see out, everyone else could see in.

Frank's profession as a record producer often took him into the recording studio late at night. Whenever he left, I was overwhelmed by the fear that someone might be standing outside the windows looking into the house. So I pulled the king-size sheets out of the closet and pinned them to the open-weave shades in six rooms. Once the sheets were in place, I'd start thinking that maybe someone was *in* the house and no one outside would be able to see in to help me. So I pulled all the sheets off the windows. Then the cycle of fear would start all over again, and those sheets would go up and down all night long. It seems silly, doesn't it? But my feelings were very real at the time.

What is your greatest fear? In what area of your life do you continue to put up and take down the sheets? Are you afraid of intruders? Confrontations? Carjackers or muggers? The I.R.S.? Financial disaster? Disease? Divorce? Death? Some of our fears are irrational and some are based on reality, which is then enhanced by our imagination. Whatever it is that frightens you, if you can identify it, you've begun the process of overcoming it.

Early in my Christian walk, the Lord showed me that my fear was misplaced. He pointed out to me that I often sinned against Him and never gave it a second thought. Yet my fear of lesser things was overwhelming. Proverbs 9:10 says, "The fear of the LORD is the beginning of wisdom...." I understood His correction, repented, and from that day forward I have walked in the knowledge that God is my protector. Psalm 4:8 states, "I will lie down and sleep in peace, for you alone, O LORD, make me dwell in safety."

Fear is rooted in the assumption that God is not in control. We feel as if we are vulnerable to life's precarious situations and unpredictable circumstances. The truth is, however, there is never a time when our God is not thinking about us. Psalm 139:17-18 (KJV) proclaims,

> *How precious to me are your thoughts, O God!*
> *How vast is the sum of them! Were I to count*
> *them, they would outnumber the grains of sand.*

If we were to pick up a handful of sand, I doubt we could even count the number of grains, let alone imagine how many grains are on every beach or ocean floor. All that immeasurable sand represents how often God thinks about us. How quickly we forget that we are His precious children.

One day I had the opportunity of putting these lessons to the test. I was making preparations for a youth conference, and it was necessary for me to meet with a printer in Los Angeles. It was broad daylight when I entered the establishment, but the meeting took longer than I expected. By the time I left, night had fallen.

I exited the building, walked around a corner, and was about halfway to my car when I noticed the streetlight was out and the sidewalk was very dark. Just then I saw two men approaching from the other direction. By the time I reached my car, one man was leaning against my car door. The other stood directly behind me. The man in front said, "Hey, baby, can I go with you?"

"No," I told him calmly. "I'm on my way home to prepare my children for Sunday school tomorrow. Do you go to church?"

He started to stutter, "Well, uh..."

I continued, "Do you know Jesus Christ as your Lord and Savior?"

By now he was beginning to move away from the car door. As he withdrew, he tried to explain that he had attended church when he was young. I put my key in the door, opened it, got in, and sat down behind the wheel. I looked at the two men and said, "Have a nice evening."

As I closed my door and drove away, I realized that I was feeling no fear. Was that because I didn't believe anything harmful could happen to me? One look at the newspapers would prove that idea untrue. And just because we're believers doesn't mean we're immune to trouble. We all know Christians who have had to suffer through tragic circumstances. Scripture teaches us that God "sends the rain on the just and on the unjust" (Matthew 5:45 NKJV).

But that incident taught me that I had come to understand perfect love casts out all fears (see 1 John 4:18).

When we accept God as sovereign and in complete control, our fears are dispelled. Giving Him full reign over our lives releases us to reach our purpose and destiny. God's Word assures us, "...all things work together for good to them that love God, to them who are the called according to his purpose" (Romans 8:28 KJV). So whatever happens to us will eventually be transformed into a testimony of God's grace.

A songwriter once wrote, "He'll turn your scars into stars, your wounds into weapons, and your mountains into gold mines." When we believe those words, our fears are removed and we are prepared to deal with any situation or circumstance we may encounter. Getting rid of our fears makes it possible for us to reach success. Like the Lion in *The Wizard of Oz*, we need to find courage. But the courage we require can only be found in the Lord.

The Spineless Scarecrow

Another character in *The Wizard of Oz* faced a different challenge. The Scarecrow had no strength, no backbone, and therefore no endurance. In short, the Scarecrow was a quitter. Now, I can relate to that.

During my senior year in high school, I worked for a physician. Next door was a psychologist's office. One day I got up nerve to ask the psychologist a question. "Why do I start projects with great enthusiasm, and then lose interest before they are finished? What concerns me most is not just that I quit, but that once I quit, I don't care anymore."

To this day, I cannot remember what he said in reply. Like most teenagers, I was more interested in talking than listening. And, whatever the answer was, it didn't solve the problem. In those days, if I'd been a racehorse and you were a betting person, you would probably put all your money on me. When I had an idea, I got excited and everybody around me got excited, too. But as soon as the gate opened and I'd galloped at full speed for a few yards, I would collapse on the track exhausted. I had no endurance.

> *"Why do I start projects with great enthusiasm, and then lose interest before they are finished?"*

In order to experience success, we have to be overcomers. Jesus says in Revelation 3:21, "To him who overcomes, I will give the right to sit with me on my throne..." Being an overcomer wasn't easy for me. If you lack endurance, take heart. If I can develop endurance, anybody can.

I think my greatest lessons in pressing through and being consistent were learned while I was raising my children. They still chuckle today as they remember living through my "plan of the week" for them. I was constantly constructing charts and graphs to keep them focused and orderly in their household chores, homework, and even playtime.

Once the chart went up on the wall, everything was perfect at least for two days. Then I would slowly begin to slip in my follow-up. Within a couple of weeks, I would be charting something new. My children suffered and I suffered. It was a hard lesson, but I learned that successful parenting demands both consistency and endurance. It requires doing the right things over and over again.

My next real education in endurance came during the writing of my first book, *Liberated Through Submission*. I had begun teaching the principle of submission at seminars. Requests for more speaking engagements became so numerous that I cried out, "Lord, I can't go to all these places and speak. My children are small and I want to be with them."

God's still, small voice replied, "Write a book, and you won't have to go anywhere."

Write a book? I thought. *I don't even like to write letters!* But the idea made sense. If I wrote down the information about submission, the message could get into the hands of thousands of people without my having to leave home.

I had never considered writing a book. I had no interest in such a venture and no training for it. I didn't have a clue as to where to begin. All of that made one thing quite obvious. The very fact I had no desire on my own to do such a thing *had* to mean that the idea hadn't come from me. So in submission to what I felt was God's directive, I began to write the first chapter. When it was complete, I put it in my dresser drawer and it stayed there for 10 years. Each time the Lord prompted me to continue, I would remind Him that I wasn't an author. One day He confirmed that to be true. He made it clear that *He* was the author and I was the coauthor, so would I please finish the book.

Fortunately I was a part of a women's fellowship which held me accountable for completing the project once I shared with them the vision. Each day I wrote for about an hour, and the two or three pages I produced continued to add up. One day, to my amazement, I had completed the manuscript. Once it was edited, the book was mailed to various publishing companies. And that brought me to my next lesson about endurance.

I was informed that it was extremely unlikely that anyone would want to read a book on submission. It seemed I had created a book that no one was interested in publishing. A friend then suggested that I publish the book myself. "Oh, great!" was my response. "First I write a book not knowing what I'm doing, and now I'm suppose to publish it myself. I don't know how to do that, either."

The process of researching self-publishing was painstaking and bothersome. But finally the pieces fell in place and *Liberated Through Submission* was printed. When I look back on it now, that book had one of the ugliest covers I have ever seen. Fortunately, despite its weaknesses, someone believed in it enough to send it to Oprah Winfrey. Oprah read the book, loved it, and invited me to be a guest on her show. Once that interview was aired, publishing companies suddenly became interested. The rest is history. When the sales of *Liberated Through Submission* exceeded 100,000 copies, I was amazed.

What I discovered during that time is that endurance begets endurance. Once you complete one thing successfully, you are in a position to breed another success. What do you feel the Lord calling you to do in your life? Do you feel inadequate and incapable? Good! Second Corinthians 12:9 says: "My grace is sufficient for thee: for my strength is made perfect in weakness" (KJV). That means you'll have to rely on the Lord to complete the project. In fact, the more impossible the task seems, the more clear it is that it wasn't your idea in the first place. God will open the necessary doors so you can move forward. You'll just need to be standing in the right place at the right time.

How should you respond to the task that God has given you? Let me encourage you to do just one thing each day toward getting it done. Make an inquiring telephone call. Write a letter. Ask a question. Make a list. Pray for direction. You will be surprised when you look up one day and discover that His assignment to you has become a reality. In fact, why not put this book down right now and begin to get something done? If I can finish what I started, believe me, you can do it, too!

Heart Trouble and the Tin Man

The poor Tin Man faced a completely different dilemma. He had no feelings and therefore he thought that he had no heart. I can understand that. In fact, if you had met me when I was in my twenties, I probably would have said something like this to you shortly after making your acquaintance: "Let me warn you about something. I suffer from a huge lack of compassion, so don't be surprised if I say something to hurt your feelings. I don't mean to. It's just the way I am."

I was like the Tin Man, believing I had no heart.

How do we come to those kinds of conclusions? We announce our shortcomings with great conviction, clinging to them, even identifying ourselves by them, as if we could never change. However, qualities like a lack of compassion are not "just the way we are." They represent the way we have been shaped. Just study a baby for a moment. She is open and trusting, completely dependent on others to take care of her and provide for her. And the way she is provided for as an infant will mold and shape her character and actions when she is older.

I had formed some misconceptions about myself. The ideas I held about my insensitivity and lack of compassion, which Satan had implanted in me during my youth, affected every relationship I had. It actually took someone who I thought was an enemy to release me from the lies I believed about myself.

Cathy (not her real name) was a part of our women's fellowship. Along with all the other women, I had informed her of my tendency to hurt people's feelings. And sure enough, one day I said something that made her angry. Cathy decided not to address it right away. Instead, she devised a plan to observe me for several months so that once she finally confronted me, she would not only have one situation to discuss, but she would have other examples to prove her point. She wanted her confrontation to have a lasting effect. Cathy intended to set me straight, once and for all.

> *We announce our shortcomings with great conviction, clinging to them, even identifying ourselves by them, as if we could never change.*

Several weeks later, she made an appointment to meet with me at my home. I could tell by her attitude that she didn't care for me, and I had no idea what to expect. Sitting across from me in my living room, Cathy announced, "You did something to me months ago that made me angry. I planned to come over here and give you numerous examples of your unkindness. I came here today, however, to tell you that I never again want to hear you say that you lack compassion and sensitivity. Like I said, I've been watching you."

Cathy then began to recount different occasions when someone in our women's fellowship had a need. She informed me of her amazement as she watched me respond to the needy person. She had noticed that I'd taken the time to care for the person and do what I could to fix the situation. "Somewhere, Bunny," she said, "you have become convinced that you don't care about people. But that is a lie. Even when I look back on what you said that offended me, I realize that you were right. You handled it in such a way as to get my attention. And it helped me overcome my problem."

After our meeting, I began to watch myself. I discovered that Cathy was right. Growing up, I had been repeatedly told that I was insensitive and lacked compassion. Like the Tin Man, I thought I had no heart. But the Bible teaches that we are made in the image of God. How can any of us be incapable of love if we are made in the image of God and God is love? We may need to learn some new habits, but we have been given the capacity—and the commandment—to love one another. Jesus said, "This is my commandment, that ye love one another, as I have loved you" (John 15:12 KJV).

What do you believe about yourself? Think back on how you were raised, and ask the Lord to reveal how much of your self-image has been falsely programmed. Psalm 139:14

teaches, "…I am fearfully and wonderfully made; your works are wonderful, I know that full well." It's important that we gain our information first and foremost from God's Word. God's encouraging voice will affirm our great value to Him, and reaffirm His love for us. Let's choose to believe God's truth about ourselves instead of putting our faith in the lies of the past.

Time and Eternity

Eternity is one of my greatest passions. I long to one day see the Savior and hear Him say, "Well done, my good and faithful servant!" And I am fascinated with the way God decided to end the Holy Bible. Have you ever thought about it?

God was so kind to condense His thoughts into one book. His Word is our blueprint for life. But the Bible needed to come to an end. Have you ever paid attention to how it was culminated? God stuck in a travel brochure! In the last two chapters of Revelation (chapters 21 and 22), God allows the Apostle John to be caught up in the spirit and to see our heavenly home.

John watched as angels measured the walls of heaven and found that they were 1,500 miles high, wide, and deep. Wow! He goes on to say that the walls of the city are made of jasper, which is clear stone. That means we can see into the city. There are 12 foundations that hold up the wall, and each one is made of a precious stone—ruby, emerald, and sapphire, among others. There are three gates on the east, west, north, and south, and each gate is made of a solid sheet of pearl. The gates are always open and no evil can enter there because an angel stands beside each gate. Don't you wonder which gate you'll be going through? What will the angel say when you arrive at the gate?

The city and the streets are pure gold, "like unto clear glass." A crystal-clear river proceeds out from underneath the throne of God and flows down through the middle of the city. Trees grow along the riverbanks and down the middle of the city, bearing 12 different fruits. Cherubim and Seraphim angels fill the heavens, where there is no hunger or thirst. And there are no more tears.

As I mentioned before, Scripture says that one day with the Lord is like a thousand years on earth. When we reflect upon the equation between eternity and earth's time, it changes our perspective. After hearing me speak, people often tell me that they feel encouraged, wanting to focus positively on the little time they have left on earth. To my dismay, however, the awareness of time versus eternity doesn't stick in their minds for long.

One day I asked the Lord, "What would remind us daily that this earth is not our final home?"

As soon as I asked the question, the picture of a fine quality wristwatch came into my mind. On the face of the watch was a gold-shaped hourglass. In the top part of the hourglass the word *Eternity* was written in gold. Below it was a diamond, but there were no hands. This represented heaven's time. In the bottom part of the hourglass was a regular watch face with golden hands. Most of us check our watches eight to ten times a day. A watch like that would help us to remember that even though we are on earth time here, before long we'll be living in eternity.

> *He will give us just enough glimpses of eternity to remind us of the shortness of our time here on earth and the glory of our future with Him.*

How beautiful! How exasperating! I could see the watch in my imagination. It was fine-quality jewelry with a genuine diamond and a leather strap. It was a timepiece an executive could wear into a boardroom. It had wonderful potential as a tool for witnessing about Jesus. But I had absolutely no idea how to bring it from the spiritual world into the natural world.

The day the Lord showed the Eternity Watch to me, I made a commitment not to wear another watch until my dream was realized. Every time I had to ask someone for the time, I was reminded of my God-given project. The success story of the Eternity Watch may help you to find a way to complete some project you've been given by God. It was seven years before I was finally wearing my Eternity Watch. Here's how it happened.

I started by making one inquiry a day. Sometimes it was a telephone call or maybe a conversation with a friend. This was before I was aware of the information superhighway or the Internet, so I had to do some research in the library. I visited large Christian bookstores that featured various jewelry lines, but found no watches remotely close to my idea. One day I was referred to a woman in New York who had distributed a Christian watch on a mass basis. I explained my idea and she quickly encouraged me not to do it. She had lost her shirt on her watch! I asked her to tell me everything she had done. I knew her information would be valuable because it would teach me what *not* to do.

It was quickly apparent that this project would be costly, so I needed a speculation investor—someone who would put money into the watch project with expectations of a high-interest return. The agreement would be based on an "if." *If* I made money, the investor would make money; if I didn't make money, neither would he. That would free me

up from the burden of a loan. Before long, a friend introduced me to a gentleman who decided to invest in the project. And he made an interesting statement when he gave me
the funds.

"Bunny," he said, "I don't know anything about watches,
and so I have no idea if this venture will work. I am not
investing in a watch; I am investing in you. All the other projects you've started have been completed, despite the obstacles you've faced."

Considering my history, that was quite an acknowledg-
ment of God's power at work in my life. I immediately
remembered that Jesus told us how important it is to be
faithful in little things. The man invested $10,000 and I
promised a 20 percent return on his money. An agreement
was drawn up, and at last I was able to produce the proposal
and a prototype of the watch. The investment also enabled
me to get a design patent approved by an attorney.

The whole process took a long time because there were
sometimes weeks when nothing happened. I would go
through every open door available until there were no more
doors in sight. Sometimes a door that I was sure was open
would close. For example, when I contacted the largest and
most successful Christian jewelry distributor on the market,
I was sure they would be impressed with my proposal and
prototype. Instead, their response was discouraging. I was
beginning to see why God did not want me to give my idea
away, but to produce it myself.

At about that time, one of my prayer partners remembered that she had a friend who was a watch collector. He put
me in touch with the president of Benrus Watch Company,
the oldest family-owned watch company in America. They
loved my idea!

Seven years after my vision of the Eternity Watch was born, the product itself was birthed. There are no words to express how I felt the first time I placed the beautiful watch on my wrist. Proverbs 13:19 says, "A longing fulfilled is sweet to the soul...". Even greater was the day I returned the investor's money—with the promised interest.

I made mistakes along the way, and there were times when it seemed as if my vision would never be fulfilled. But I had to continue to remind myself it was not *my* project. God had given it to me, and it was *His* responsibility to bring it to pass. My responsibility was to be faithful and not quit. What sheer delight it is for me to one day see someone wearing an Eternity Watch!

Let's reflect back on *The Wizard of Oz*. Just as Dorothy eventually returned to Kansas—with God's help—we can find our way to our destination. God can help us to achieve success with the things He gives us to do. And ultimately, when our lives on earth are over, we will find ourselves home, enjoying the beautiful scenery of heaven.

What can we learn from Dorothy and her friends? That the Lord will give us the courage we need to move forward. He will provide us with the endurance necessary to complete our tasks. He will tell us the truth about ourselves, and keep lies and deception from crippling us. Best of all, He will give us just enough glimpses of eternity to remind us of the shortness of our time here on earth and the glory of our future with Him. He has prepared for us an eternal home that exceeds anything we could dream of. And that home is waiting for us far, far beyond the Yellow Brick Road.

Chapter Six Workbook

Reflection:

What is your greatest fear(s)? (For the sake of privacy you may just want to think about this and not write it down. But do think about it.) How do you plan to overcome it (them)?

Meditation:

Scripture Memory:
"I will both lay me down in peace, and sleep:
for thou, O LORD, only makest me dwell in safety"
(Psalm 4:8 KJV).

"To him who overcomes, I will give
the right to sit with me on my throne..."
(Revelation 3:21).

"My grace is sufficient for thee,
for my strength is made perfect in weakness"
(2 Corinthians 12:9 KJV).

Response:

What desire or project do you have on your heart? Begin today by just doing one thing; a phone call, an inquiry, or a conversation is a start. Chart your progress.

7
Love Never Fails

I choose to practice sacrificial love...

*L*et me ask you a very important question. Does someone in your life seem impossible to love? Think about it for a moment. Maybe it's a family member who causes you nothing but trouble. Maybe it's a coworker who makes your life miserable. Maybe it's an egotistical church member or a trouble-making neighbor. Sad to say, maybe it's even your husband.

Now what would you think if I told you that that person is a precious gift from God? Believe it or not, that's true. Difficult relationships help us mature in our faith. They make it possible for us to accumulate a great reward in heaven, which will be awaiting us once we find victory in the relationship. They help us to understand the fifth Secret every woman needs to know—the secret of practicing Sacrificial Love.

God's Word promises, "Love never fails" (1 Corinthians 13:8). It also assures us, "...love is as strong as death..." (Song of Songs 8:6). And as we know, death is irreversible. God's love is expressed in the Greek language as *agape*, which means that it is unconditional, and it should be a goal of

ours to reach out in unconditional love to those around us—
the good, the bad, and the worst. What better way for us to
demonstrate the incredible *agape* love of Christ who died on
the cross for us while we were yet sinners?

Have you ever received unconditional love from another
person? What we eventually discover is that most of the love
we receive in our lives is very conditional. And it's our
human nature to return the same kind of love. What another
person does for us, or how we are treated by them, usually
directly affects the way we respond to them. But Jesus had a
different kind of love in mind for us. He said, "Love your
enemies and pray for those who persecute you, that you may
be sons of your Father in heaven. He causes his sun to rise on
the evil and the good.... If you love those who love you, what
reward will you get?" (Matthew 5:44-46).

Difficult relationships help us mature in our faith.

In my book *Betrayal's Baby*, I describe my own journey
into unconditional love. Only my intense commitment to
God kept me on the right path. My challenge focused around
relationships with my stepdaughter, my mother, and one of
my daughters. For the most part, the greatest struggle—which
spanned about three years—took place all at one time. I shed
a lot of tears because I caused much of the pain myself. I had
not yet addressed many issues from the past, and my
responses to situations flowed out of some unfinished business in my heart.

Eventually, as I came to understand the source of my bitterness, the problems were resolved. And today, each encounter
I have with those three precious people is bathed in gratitude.

I remember where we once were, and I know very well where we could have ended up. What a loss it would have been if I had not learned to walk in *agape*, and in the forgiving footsteps of Jesus. I had to make a conscious decision to forgive myself for the things I had done to those people. And I had to then forgive them for what I perceived they had done to me.

When I answered the telephone the other day, I was delighted to hear my mother's voice on the other end. We chatted about this and that, and when the conversation came to an end, she signed off with, "I love you." The genuineness in her voice caused tears to come to my eyes as I recalled the days when we shared no communication. The change didn't happen overnight. There were many days when it seemed as if no progress had been made, or worse yet, that we were moving backwards.

The holidays were once difficult times for me, often marred by smart side comments intended to shoot straight into the heart. Now those are my favorite times of the year, times when our family comes together and the spirit of peace rests upon our fellowship. Jesus has paid the price of peace, so we are free to love one another.

Unconditional love is the most powerful weapon on earth. What a joy it has been for me to taste the sweet victory which comes with its application. But perhaps an even greater joy is the privilege of assuring you that unconditional love can touch your life, too. I can bear personal witness that God's Word is true: Love never fails.

A Love Song

One night during a gospel concert, I was mesmerized by by a singer's testimony of his mother's unconditional love for him. Adopted by an elderly woman, he became rebellious as he grew into his teenage years. His mother believed in prayer and continued to trust God for her son's deliverance. I'm sure his wild lifestyle was a disappointment to her, but she remained steadfast in her unconditional love.

One day, he felt impressed to go by his mother's home. When she didn't answer the door, he immediately sensed that something was wrong. He went around to her bedroom window, looked inside, and saw that she was in the bed. He kept knocking, but she did not respond.

When the police arrived and broke into the house, they discovered that his mother was dead. The young man's heart was wrenched with regret and remorse. His life was deeply impacted by the passing of this precious woman, who had continued to love him no matter what he did. He has gone on to become one of the greatest gospel performers of all times and has since led many others into a saving knowledge of Jesus Christ.

When his mother took her last breath, she had not seen her prayers answered. But she stepped into her eternal home, and someday he will join her there. Once again, the Bible is proven true when it says, "Love never fails."

Rachel's Tough Love

Unconditional love isn't always a matter of prayer, kind gestures, and patience. Sometimes it has to be accompanied by restraint and discipline in order to help the object of our love find his or her way out of a maze of sin. Although the names have been changed, the following story is true.

After speaking at a women's conference at an outdoor amphitheater, I was approached by a woman and her 15-year-old daughter. Both were crying. The mother tried her best to hurry through her life's story, afraid she was taking up too much of my time. Toward the end, she placed a beautiful, hardbound children's book in my hands. It was a book she had written herself, and with gratitude she explained how at my last conference I had stimulated her to pursue her dream of writing. I was so touched by her testimony that I invited her and her three children to visit me at our home.

It was not long thereafter that Rachel and her daughter Melanie were sitting in my backyard, pouring out their hearts. Rachel had been a stay-at-home mom, married to Paul, a responsible father who had been actively involved in the family's church. Eighteen years into the marriage, Paul was involved in a work-related accident. When a building caught on fire, he went back in to save another man, and the chemicals in the air burned his lungs. What ensued were endless days and nights in the hospital. Paul's prolonged illness and physical pain eventually affected his temperament.

> *She wrote a heartrending letter to her father and ended it with, "I don't know who you are. When you see my daddy, would you tell him I love him?"*

As the family income dwindled and the medical bills continued to soar, Rachel was forced to seek employment outside the home for the first time in her life. Meanwhile, her husband seemed to have become a recluse. The once-active head of the home became more and more withdrawn as he battled with tremendous bouts of discomfort. Rachel continued to love him unconditionally, but to no avail. Her love couldn't seem to reach him.

One day Rachel came home and discovered that Paul was moving out. He told her that she deserved better. "My life is jinxed," he said. She later discovered that Paul had moved in with another woman he met at work. Rachel and the children were devastated. Melanie, who had been her Daddy's little princess, particularly agonized over this new turn of events. She wrote a heartrending letter to her father and ended it with, "I don't know who you are. When you see my daddy, would you tell him I love him?"

As Rachel recounted the details of her family's heartbreaking loss, I wept. Here sat a woman whose life was unexplainably shattered, yet it was clear that she had determined to hold no animosity toward the man who had caused all of her anguish. Melanie, on the other hand, was seething with bitterness. She was even angry at her mother's unconditional love toward her father.

As we sat in my backyard, I asked Rachel, "What if Paul wanted to come back home?"

Rachel pondered the question and answered, "I don't know. I don't see that happening."

Two days later I received a telephone call from Rachel.

"Bunny," she said, "you're not going to believe this. Paul came to pick up the boys and asked if he could speak to me alone. We went out on the front porch, and he told me how sorry he was for all the pain he's caused. He said he wants to come back home!"

"Rachel," I prodded, "what did you tell him?"

"Well," she answered, "at first I didn't know what to say. There was this uncomfortable silence, and I asked God to direct me. When I opened my mouth, my response was this. I explained that if I was going to allow him to come home, he had to first apologize to the children. Next we would need to meet with our pastor. Then we would have to enter counseling for a year before he could come back into the house.

He's been gone a year, and it would take that long for me to know that he has been emotionally healed."

"Good for you!" I declared.

Rachel allowed God to lead her into a tough-love approach to fixing her relationship with Paul, an approach that was intended to nurture his healing. She threw him a lifeline, and it would be up to him to grab it.

Melanie, on the other hand, was furious. She couldn't understand how her mother would even consider allowing her father to return home. He had left them all without offering financial support. He had repeatedly promised to visit the children, and then came late or not at all. He had allowed the medical bills to become Rachel's sole responsibility.

When Paul first left home, Rachel had been unskilled in career-type work and had no idea how she could carry the entire financial load. Before long, however, a man in her church offered her a position in his company as his personal assistant. He sent her to secretarial school and trained her personally. Rachel had known him and his wife for several years, but could not understand why he chose to employ her. When she asked, he explained, "I watched you over all the years when you took care of your husband. I needed an assistant with more than skill. I knew you could learn the details of the job, but the qualities you possess as a person can't be taught."

Soon Rachel was making enough to meet her family's monthly expenses. But the weight of the medical bills still proved to be too much of a burden. Finally, she had to make the heart-wrenching decision to file for bankruptcy.

As she waited in the courtroom, she watched the two cases before hers. In both cases, the judge was abrupt and insulting to the people involved. But when Rachel's turn came, after he reviewed the file, he looked up over his horn-rimmed glasses and spoke to her as if he were her father.

"Rachel," he said, "you are the kind of person for which the bankruptcy courts were created. I hope this will help you get a new start on life."

As Rachel drove home, she thought about the people from whom she had received personal loans. It grieved her to think that she could not repay them. She cried out to God, "Father, if I had $20,000, I could pay off all my personal debts."

When Rachel returned home, she found a check for $20,000 in the mail, sent to her by an anonymous donor.

If you're like me, you're probably wondering if Paul came home. The answer is no. He refused to get counseling, so he didn't grab his lifeline. And Melanie still has some work to do in her own heart, dealing with her bitterness and unforgiveness.

But Rachel's testimony is a story of unconditional love. She was stripped of her material securities, betrayed by her husband, and left to raise her children alone. Yet she has not allowed herself to become bitter. When I talk to Rachel, I am always deeply affected by her joy and her enthusiasm for life. She moves in the knowledge and appreciation that God is her husband. I believe if the Bible were being written today, Rachel would have a chapter in it.

How will this story end? Even without knowing the details, we know that God's promise to Rachel will remain true to the end: "Love never fails."

The Story of Poor Mike

I don't know about you, but stories that demonstrate the power of unconditional love lift my heart. Here's another one. A nationally renowned speaker told about her son-in-law's early years. The young man grew up in a home with an alcoholic father. Every weekend, the father would go out drinking until almost all of his weekly wages were spent. When he finally staggered home, his wife met him on the front porch and said, "Poor Mike, you look terrible. Come in the house so I can take care of you."

After giving Mike a bath and putting him to bed, his wife tended to the needs of her six sons. The family was so poor that the mother sometimes cut up her dresses in order to sew shirts for her boys. But she never said a negative thing about Mike. And whenever her sons started to express anger about their father, she said, "Alcohol is bad, but your father is a good man. Let's pray for him."

Years passed, and every one of the woman's sons grew into a man who loved the Lord. Some became preachers, some became deacons, and some held other positions of authority in the church.

And after years of prayer, Mike finally surrendered his life to the Lord and became a deacon in the church. All the while, this woman refused to allow bitterness to enter her own heart or the hearts of her sons. She has spent a lifetime loving her husband unconditionally, and at last she is reaping the benefits. One of her six sons married the daughter of that nationally renowned speaker. Despite the hardships of this man's childhood, he is an excellent husband and father. Why? Because "love never fails."

> *"Alcohol is bad, but your father is a good man.*
> *Let's pray for him."*

Always and Forever

One of the best ways unconditional love can be seen is in a person's relationship with an Alzheimer's patient. I was deeply moved one day when I heard this testimony on James Dobson's radio program. An elderly woman shared about the intense love she and her husband of many years had shared. When he first developed Alzheimer's, his memory would go in and out. At times he still recognized her, but his condition continued to grow worse and finally he had no recollection of the past or of loved ones.

One evening as this woman crawled into bed, her husband became very upset. He said, "You can't get in this bed. Only my wife can sleep here."

This precious saint made her way to the couch in the living room and, lying there, she rejoiced in her heart. It blessed her to know that even in her husband's illness, he had remained faithful to her.

This woman's husband will probably die and not remember the tremendous time, love, and energy that went into making his life pleasant in his latter years. It is an unconditional *agape* love that propels a person to serve someone on that level.

Some people have Alzheimer's in their physical body, but I also believe that some suffer from similar symptoms emotionally. They don't know or have forgotten the goodness of God, and they dwell in a place called Bitterness. They are very difficult to love because they so quickly forget the positive things others have done for them. Even so, "love never fails."

And What About You?

These stories of unconditional love are real. Love never fails *when we do it God's way*. What is your love story? What unconditional love situation are you facing? Are you living in anger and bitterness over the actions of another person? Have you taken the step of faith to love that person unconditionally and sacrificially, even if you sometimes have to exercise tough love?

Sacrificial love causes us to place our emotions and stipulations on God's altar as we line up with His instructions. And in case you are wondering what unconditional love looks like, 1 Corinthians 13 says:

> *If I speak in the tongues of men and of angels,*
> *but have not love, I am only a resounding gong*
> *or a clanging cymbal. If I have the gift of prophecy*
> *and can fathom all mysteries and all knowledge,*
> *and if I have faith that can move mountains, but*
> *have not love, I am nothing. If I give all I possess*
> *to the poor and surrender my body to the flames,*
> *but have not love, I gain nothing. Love is patient,*
> *love is kind. It does not envy, it does not boast, it*
> *is not proud. It is not rude, it is not self-seeking, it*
> *is not easily angered, it keeps no record of wrongs.*
> *Love does not delight in evil but rejoices with the*
> *truth. It always protects, always trusts, always*
> *hopes, always perseveres. Love never fails (verses*
> *1-8).*

I hope you don't think you're going to get out of this life without having to deal with at least one unconditional love experience.

Love is its own reward.

"But, Bunny," you may be saying, "I could handle *one* situation. However, I have a whole barrel full of them."

Good! The more the merrier. Start one at a time. Pick the hardest one, because you probably feel the weakest in that situation. And, as we've already discovered, God's strength is made perfect in our weakness (see 2 Corinthians 12:9).

Our goal is not to look for results. When we do that, we are often tempted to slip back into our bitterness. Peace comes from the very act of *unconditional* love. Exercising that principle allows our heavenly Father to put things in motion within the spiritual realm.

We always need to remind ourselves that God's timing is not our timing. Remember the Eternity Watch? He does not work according to our earthly clock. At the very beginning, we need to make the decision that, no matter how everything turns out and no matter how long it takes, we will allow the Lord as much time and space as He needs to do His work. It's a good idea to have a prayer partner who fully agrees with our decision to practice sacrificial love, because things may not always go the way we want them to. How grateful I am that on my most discouraging days, my husband, Frank, always reminded me that love is its own reward.

Our job is not to determine the outcome of a situation or relationship. Our only responsibility is to keep our hearts tender with forgiveness, compassion, and unconditional love. Even when external circumstances seem to declare failure, our heart's cry should be, "God, please give me more *agape* love!" Even when tough love needs to be applied, our main focus should always be the condition of our hearts. Only God's love should motivate our actions.

As I write this chapter, I am so thankful for the work God has done in my heart. By His grace alone, I cannot think of one broken relationship in my life. There may be some I don't know about, but once I had been made aware, I would respond immediately. And there are no words to express the peace that abides in my heart because of this.

Why is sacrificial love one of the Seven Secrets every woman needs to know? Because a price tag can never be placed on the powerful, transformative love of God and the miracles it can accomplish. Think about those "unlovable" people in your life. Commit to applying *agape* love to each of them. If you have not already done so, launch out into the deep. There will be a life preserver waiting for you. And on it, you'll find an inscription which says, "Love never fails."

Chapter Seven Workbook

Reflection:

Who in your life seems impossible to love?

Meditation:

Scripture Memory:
"Love never fails"
(1 Corinthians 13:8).

"Love is as strong as death"
(Song of Songs 8:6).

"...for my strength is made perfect in weakness"
(2 Corinthians 12:9 KJV).

Response:

Once you have identified your "impossible to love" person, it is now time to respond. If you feel you need extra encouragement, read my book *Betrayal's Baby.* If not, you have a visit or phone call to make. Go with a heart for there to be peace in the relationship. Don't have any expectations. Simply be obedient to God.

8

Pruned to Bloom

I realize that my sacrificial love may cause suffering...

ave you ever met anyone who has not suffered in some way? I haven't. Even those who have perfect health, are financially secure, enjoy good family relationships, and are successful, still suffer when they see the plight of others around them. Just watching the evening news and seeing the grim results of international violence, starvation, racism, "ethnic cleansing" and murder can (and should) be a great source of suffering. On a more personal level, if we're believers, we suffer as we fight to control our thought life and continuously battle against our flesh, which is always trying to control us. Jesus assured us that we would suffer when He said, "In this world you will have trouble" (John 16:33). Suffering is a fact of life. We see it clearly in Galatians 5:22-23: "But the fruit of the Spirit is love, joy, peace, *longsuffering*, gentleness, goodness, faith, meekness, temperance [self-control]" (KJV). Having said all that, however, there is a marked difference between suffering with and without Christ.

Over the years, the Lord has illustrated His principles to me by bringing to my mind word pictures and parables. The following story was written to demonstrate why. In James 1:2, God's Word reminds us to "Consider it pure joy, my brothers, whenever you face trials of many kinds...."

Vines and Branches

> *The vine pulled her leaves back and pleaded,*
> *"Why are you doing this? Haven't I been sweet?*
> *Didn't I bring honor to the garden? Please, no!*
> *Don't do this to me!"*

Once upon a time, there was an old grapevine which had been growing in a vineyard for a very long time. One day, a new vine was planted in the next row over. It grew, developed branches, and bore fruit.

Taking courage one hot summer day, the young vine looked up at the old vine and said in its squeaky voice, "It must be great to have people travel from miles around just to taste the sweetness of your fruit."

The old vine nodded.

Feeling encouraged, the young vine continued. "I've been talking with the other vines in the garden, and they say yours is the sweetest fruit."

The old vine smiled.

"When I grow up, I want to be just like you! If you'll tell me what to do, I promise to be determined and committed."

The old vine looked down on the young branch and reminisced about a conversation years before when he had asked another old vine the same question. Giving the young vine the same answer he had once received, he replied in a deep voice, "Be willing."

The young vine mused in frustration and said to himself, "Be willing? *Be willing?* I tell him I'm determined and committed, and he says, 'Be willing'? He's probably just having a bad day!"

Every day in the garden there was constant chatter as the vines shared the latest gossip and wasted the hours away by bragging about the sweetness of their fruit. The young vine knew there was no other place he'd rather live.

One cool autumn morning, the young vine was awakened by the opening creak of the weathered brown gate. He looked down toward the end of the row. In stepped the gardener. But something unusual was happening that day. Any other time when the gardener came to visit, the vines all clapped their leaves together and shouted praises and adoration to him. But this time a silent hush fell across the vineyard.

The gardener stopped by one particular vine, which had always seemed to please him. As the young vine watched intently, he saw the gardener bend on one knee, reach into his back pocket, and pull out what looked like sharp scissors.

The vine pulled her leaves back and pleaded, "No, no, why are you doing this? Haven't I been sweet? Didn't I bring honor to the garden? Please, please, no! Don't do this to me!"

But before the vine could blink, her branches lay on the ground. The young vine turned to the old one and asked in a low, fearful voice, "What's happening? Why did the gardener do that?"

The old vine did not respond.

"Oh, I get it. This is a teaching thing, right? I told you I was determined and committed, and you want me to figure this thing out for myself. That's it, isn't it? Okay, but when I guess it, you have to tell me if I'm right!"

The young branch paused for a moment, trying to understand, and then blurted out his guess. "We thought the gardener liked that vine, but he really didn't like her after all, did he?"

The old branch responded, "No, what you just saw the gardener do proves that he loves her very much."

"I knew that. Let me try again. We thought that vine's fruit was sweet, but it really wasn't sweet after all."

"That vine's fruit was wonderfully sweet."

"Okay, those were just two guesses. This is the real reason. That branch did something wrong so the gardener is punishing her. He's just not telling us why."

The old vine answered, "That branch is not being punished; she's being *pruned*. He isn't pruning her because she was trying to do it wrong, but because she was trying to do it right. He's not doing it because her fruit was not sweet, but because the gardener wants it to be sweeter."

"But that's not fair!" announced the young vine. "Just look at her. She's been cut down to the nub. She looks awful. Now all the people who come around to taste the sweetness of her fruit will laugh. They'll think her fruit is bad."

"Only those outside the garden who don't understand the process will laugh and judge the fruit."

"Only those outside the garden who don't understand? That vine didn't understand! Did you hear her say, 'Why are you doing this to me?'"

The old vine was quiet for a long time, and then responded slowly. "Unfortunately, what you are saying is true. It's one thing when observers outside the garden don't understand, but when they are inside the garden it causes a lot of confusion, disappointment, and pain. Those vines down at the end of the row will have to listen to her murmur and complain until she puts forth new branches and blooms again."

The young vine proclaimed, "Well, *you* don't have to worry about being pruned. You have the sweetest fruit in the garden!"

"I want to be pruned," the old vine said quietly.

"You *what*? Are you crazy? For one thing, it hurts. For another, you're going to look bad."

The old vine chuckled and replied, "I must admit that it's quite uncomfortable. And I know, my young friend, that I look good to you. But I have a fungus growing on my underside which no one can see. If it remains, it will diminish the quality and quantity of my fruit. No, when the gardener comes to prune me, I won't pull back my branches. I'll lift them high in the air to make his job easier."

Trembling, the young vine responded, "I don't understand."

With compassion, the old branch replied, "My young friend, did you see that branch the gardener just tore off and threw over the fence? It didn't belong in this garden and will be burned in a fire."

"Wow!"

"When the gardener comes to prune you, remember these four things. First, the gardener only prunes those who belong to him, which makes it an honor. Second, pruning doesn't happen because you're trying to do things wrong, but because you're trying to do things right. Third, it doesn't happen because you're not sweet, but because the gardener wants you to be sweeter. And finally, always remember my young friend, *the very fact you're being pruned means you will bloom again."*

> An incurable fungus attaches itself to the branches. The only way to treat it is to cut the branches off. But each time the vine is pruned, its fruit grows sweeter.

Just then the gardener stopped next to the old vine, and the young vine watched as his friend raised his leaves high in the air. He heard a snip, and several of the old vine's branches lay on the ground. Then the gardener turned to the young vine. His leaves were shaking and tears rolled down his trunk, but with every ounce of strength he raised his branches high in the air. Then he looked up in the gardener's face and said, "Kind and gentle gardener, I am willing."

The Secret to Bearing Good Fruit

In John 15:1-2, Jesus says, "I am the true vine, and my Father is the gardener. He cuts off every branch in me that bears no fruit, while every branch that does bear fruit he prunes so that it will be even more fruitful."

Isn't it just like God to use an earthly example to explain a spiritual principle? In an earthly vineyard, pruning is the most important gardening function. It takes place annually, and up to 90 percent of each vine is cut away in the process. Pruning positively affects the quantity and quality of the vine's fruit.

Grapevine branches are constantly attacked by diseases, which can sometimes be kept at bay by pesticides and insecticides. But the vine *has* to be pruned because of an incurable fungus that attaches itself to the branches. The only way to treat it is to cut the branches off. And each time the vine is pruned, its fruit grows sweeter.

When the Apostle talks about *fruit* in John 15:1-2, to what is he referring? A Greek study into that word "fruit" reveals that it means our Christian disposition, attitude, and temperament. How do we respond when we are pruned? That discloses our true level of spiritual growth.

Since we have given our hearts to Jesus, are we sweeter? Do we make a sincere attempt to do what is right? Even with all our efforts, are we perfect? Of course not. The very fact we have not reached perfection means we will be pruned—regularly. And just like that old grapevine, we need to grow to a place where we want to be pruned, as uncomfortable as that may be. We should be willing to readily expose the fungus that grows on our underside so that our motivations and meditations are kept pure.

What do I mean when I use the word "pruning"? Pruning can come in many forms. It can be the consequences of our behavior. It can be injustice brought upon us by another. It can look like a streak of bad luck (although serious Christians don't believe in "luck"). It can be sickness. It can be betrayal. It can be disappointment, discouragement, or disillusionment. God can use anything difficult, painful, or challenging to prune us.

Pruning usually doesn't happen without others knowing about it. And one of the greatest challenges we face when we are pruned is the spirit of condemnation. There are those who will suggest that something is wrong with us unless we are in full bloom all the time. When was the last time you were going through a struggle and a friend came up to you with words of encouragement?

It may have been awhile since you heard someone say, "I've been watching you. I know you are trying to do things right. I can see that you're continuing to grow in your relationship with the Lord. I just want to encourage you that this difficult time will pass, and you'll be better for it. I'll walk with you through it." Like the old grapevine would say to the young one, "Don't worry, you're just being *pruned to bloom.*"

Unfortunately, more often than not, instead of encouragement, we are given a specific list of all the things we're doing wrong. We're told that that's why God is "punishing" us. People will advise us that we don't pray enough, fast enough, or have faith enough. Or they'll question whether God is exacting revenge for one of our shortcomings. So on top of being cut down to the nub, we also sit under the condemnation of our well-meaning friends. That by-product of the pruning process is oftentimes the most painful of all.

We usually find ourselves in one of three places—we have just been pruned, we are growing after a pruning, or we are in full bloom. Perhaps, right at the moment, everything is going well in your life. Enjoy yourself and be thankful, but remember that because you are not perfect, you will be pruned again. That knowledge will keep you humble during blooming season.

It could be that you are growing again after a pruning. Your regrowth will be stunted if you spend your time looking back on your last pruning with regret instead of gratitude. It may be tempting to walk in unforgiveness and bitterness over the unpleasant event that took place. Instead of seeing it as a problem, see it as a pruning and let it go. Then rejoice that you've gained the strength to grow richer foliage and to bear better fruit.

Maybe you have just recently been pruned and you've been cut down to the nub. You know you look bad, and you are still in pain. Be patient, and the pain will pass. Rejoice that the fungus has been cut away, and rest assured that in time you will bloom again. Don't stunt your growth with, "What if...?" or "If I had only..." Stop asking God, "Why?" Instead, thank Him for His infinite wisdom. He is the Master Gardener, and He knows what is best for you. You'll discover your discomfort quickly diminishing.

That Incurable Fungus

As with grapevines, there's a fungus that persistently attaches itself to our spiritual underside and appears in the most peculiar places. That insidious intruder is self—our flesh, our natural desire, which insists on having its own way. Our old, fleshly sin nature never goes away. It will be with us until we die. No matter how much we love the Lord, the sin fungus will always be present. It is incurable and often undetected by the human eye. Galatians 5:17 says, "For the flesh lusts against the Spirit, and the Spirit against the flesh; and these are contrary to one another..." (NKJV).

Our natural self will always cause us to suffer because its intent is to rob us of God's best plans for our lives. And the more we surrender to it, the more we turn our hearts away from the Lord and toward self-satisfaction. We have to learn to readily recognize self so we can respond to its lustful nature quickly and slow our pruning process down. First Corinthians 11:31 says, "...if we judged ourselves, we would not come under judgment."

Self can usually be identified by what we are trying to control and what is controlling us. In one instance we are playing God, in the other we are refusing to believe that there is a God who will help us. Take a moment and ask yourself a couple of questions. Are you desperately trying to stay in control of something in your life? What is it that you're trying to control?

If you are single, are you attempting to determine when and how you will meet "Mr. Right"? Are you frustrated, despondent, and despairing? Then you are trying to be in control. It is important to remember that for every *godly* single person who *desires* a godly spouse, there is one. But the emphasis is on the words *godly* and *desire*. Godly is when you don't want to break God's heart. You would deny yourself rather than knowingly go against His will. And true desire is when you allow God to place His desire in your heart for your life. If His desire for you is marriage, He will then answer His own desire. *He* will make it happen in His time and in His way. Frustration is replaced by patient anticipation, knowing that the Lord is in control.

Maybe you are a single parent and are trying to control (manipulate) your child or children. If so, you are probably near the end of your rope. If you're a woman, the Lord created you to be the nurturer. That doesn't mean, however, that you forsake the discipline. It suggests that you should be very definite about your guidelines and tremendously consistent in your response to those directions. That will leave time for nurturing your children, building them up, and edifying their potential with your love.

You may be separated from your husband, which in most cases means that you are in a terrible state of mind. You are being pulled between two forces, one determined to end the marriage, and the other trying to hold on to the possibility that it may work out. Let me encourage you to release the situation into the Lord's hand. If your husband wants a divorce, he doesn't need his mind changed; he needs his heart fixed. And only God can do that.

Most women I have met who are separated from their husbands are not thinking about getting involved with another man. That's good, because it gives God the opportunity He needs to work things out in His way and His time. When you relax and give your circumstances to the Lord, you will respond differently when you are around your husband. God will be free to control your conversations and actions. Don't get ahead of God or try to tell Him what to do. Just live in quiet assurance that He has the situation under control.

> *When the devil attacks us, his intention is destruction. When God prunes us, His intent is distinction—bigger growth and sweeter fruit. It's important to know the difference.*

Maybe your area of control involves your work. Maybe you're struggling in your church activities. Maybe it's your weight or your parents or your finances or your dreams for the future that you're trying to manage. No matter how good your goals may be, when you can no longer say, "Thy will be done" to God, and you think you have to make everything work out all by yourself, you'll probably soon find yourself being pruned.

The self fungus will never leave us alone while on earth. It will constantly try to attach itself to our lives, and we must fervently fight against it. Many times it is aggravated by our archenemy, the devil. That's why God's Word warns us in 1 Peter 5:8, "Be self-controlled and alert. Your enemy the devil prowls around like a roaring lion looking for someone to devour."

When the devil attacks us, his intention is destruction. When God prunes us, His intent is distinction—bigger growth and sweeter fruit. It's important to know the difference. As believers, we must understand that Satan can ask God's permission to hurt us in some way, but he only has the power to do so if God allows it. Isn't it wonderful to know that the devil isn't free to do anything he wants to us? Otherwise, we would probably all be sick or dead! Do you remember the story of Job? It is a perfect picture of just how far Satan can go in touching God's people. Job 1:6-12 reads:

> *One day the angels came to present themselves before the LORD, and Satan also came with them. The LORD said to Satan, "Where have you come from?"*
>
> *Satan answered the LORD, "From roaming through the earth and going back and forth in it."*
>
> *Then the LORD said to Satan, "Have you considered my servant Job? There is no one on earth like him; he is blameless and upright, a man who fears God and shuns evil."*
>
> *"Does Job fear God for nothing?" Satan replied. "Have you not put a hedge around him and his household and everything he has? You have blessed the work of his hands, so that his flocks and herds are spread throughout the land. But stretch out your hand and strike everything he has, and he will surely curse you to your face."*
>
> *The LORD said to Satan, "Very well, then, everything he has is in your hands, but on the man himself do not lay a finger."*

If you have never read the book of Job, please take the time to do so. It is full of wonderful truth about the Lord's dealing with Satan and His relationship with Job, one of His most faithful followers. You'll learn about Job's endurance and, finally, about his restoration. As you can see from Job's story, Satan must *first* get permission.

And even when he gets permission, God still has the last word. That's why Romans 8:28 says: "And we know that in all things God works for the good of those who love him...." God's Word doesn't say that all things *feel* good. It says that all things *work* for good. Paul also wrote, in verse 18 of the same chapter, "I consider that our present sufferings are not worth comparing with the glory that will be revealed in us."

A Recent Pruning

Can you remember your last pruning? Boy, I sure can! As a matter of fact, it happened while I was writing this chapter. It is a clear illustration of the type of challenges we will face until we get to heaven.

Frank and I had just finished our Master's Degree Seminar at a large church in central California. The seminar material is taken from our book by the same name, and in the course we challenge couples to treat their marriage as if it were a university and their spouse were their major. We encourage couples to "enroll" in their spouse and to take classes in communication, finances, sex, spiritual maturity, and other relevant subjects. Our goal is to help them graduate *cum laude* instead of "Lawdy, how come?" It is for singles, too, because we believe the time for singles to get information about marriage is *before* they get married.

It had been a successful three days. You could see the spirit of hope coursing through the lives of both single and married attendees. Marriages on the brink of divorce were snatched out of the jaws of Satan. We were rejoicing.

Frank taught two sessions on Saturday morning and then played 12 holes of golf. By evening he was very, very tired. But we had made a commitment to go to dinner with eight couples who were in leadership at the host church.

Frank did not realize it, but this was the same city where I had addressed women at a stadium event and the Lord had moved in a very powerful way. My message had been on the subject of servanthood, and during the presentation I had encouraged married women with children to slow their schedules down. I told them, if at all possible, to come out of the workplace and stay home so they could better serve their husband and children. I had told about the large number of speaking engagement requests I receive each year and how I had made the decision to schedule only one out-of-town personal speaking engagement a month. I had even shared about the daily tea times I had with each of my children when they came home from school. There had been a tremendous response to my message.

Now six months later, some of the same women who had been at my presentation the year before were with us at the dinner. Several of them had worked on the stadium event, and most had heard my message that morning reemphasizing the importance of spending time with their families. During dinner, someone at the table asked Frank to share the scope of his work.

He talked about the minstry of the Christians Entertainer's Fellowship, our youth ministry, and counseling of people in leadership. He also mentioned his position as superintendent of the church school department, his availability to critique the music of Christians in the secular music and film industry, and *Dayspring*, our annual Christian growth conference. In addition, he also made reference to his music and book writings. When he mentioned that his schedule limits the amount of speaking engagements he can accept, he casually remarked, "But, of course, Bunny is gone all the time."

I was stunned. Softly, I responded, "No, Frank, I only do one personal out-of-town speaking engagement a month."

Frank continued, "No, she's gone all the time," and continued talking. He didn't realize that his lighthearted remarks had seriously wounded me. I felt like a grapevine that had been cut down to the nub.

As I mentioned before, the word "fruit" in John 15:1-2 means our Christian attitude, character, and disposition. Not many years before, I would have addressed the issue right then and there at the dinner table. I would have made sure Frank got it straight before we left. Or I would have waited until we returned to our room to blow up. I did neither. I went to bed, slept all night, and didn't address the situation for two days. That's not to say it wasn't on my mind. I just knew I was too upset to be gracious; I needed first to take it to the Lord and bathe it in prayer.

Two days passed. On the third day, after my morning prayer, I took Frank's hand, led him to our office, and poured my heart out to him. I didn't do it in anger or frustration, but in honest pain. I explained how what he said discredited my testimony given the year before, as well as my recent teachings to the women at the Master's Degree Seminar. In essence, he had made me appear to be a liar. I wept as I expressed my concern that my Christian witness might have been damaged.

Dear, sweet Frank listened patiently, then put his arms around me and held me close. He began to pray and acknowledged his error to God. Later that day, he handed me a two-page letter which he had written to the woman in charge of the women's ministry at the church we had just left. In the letter, Frank explained his intent, and how the things I had taught were basically true; he pointed out that his seemingly casual remark had cast me in an untrue light. Frank went on to highlight some of my actions concerning my commitment to him and to my family.

> *He didn't realize that his lighthearted remarks had seriously wounded me. I felt like a grapevine that had been cut down to the nub.*

As you can see, my pruning came unintentionally at the hands of a loved one. I was humiliated. But in hindsight, I rejoiced to see how I had grown in my Christian attitude, temperament, and disposition. God worked it all out to His glory. To this day, I am grateful.

How did you do at your last pruning? Whether it came at the hands of a loved one, a coworker, a friend, or an enemy, were you pleased with your response? More than that, was God pleased? If yes, be encouraged and fortified because there will be another pruning in the future. If you didn't do so well, then commit to do better next time.

Suffering—long-suffering—is a matter of fact in the lives of all Christians. And it's one of the Secrets every woman wants to know. Instead of trying to avoid it, let's welcome the Gardener when He comes through the vineyard gate with His shears. Let's be like the young grapevine that raised its branches in the air and said, "Kind and gentle Gardener, I am willing."

Chapter Eight Workbook

Reflection:

Up until the time you read this chapter, did you know that pruning was a regular event in the life of a Christian? If you didn't know, reflect on your last pruning. How did you respond? If your response was not good, are you ready to get your heart right?

Meditation:

Scripture Memory:
*"I am the true vine, and my Father is the gardener.
He cuts off every branch in me that bears no fruit,
while every branch that does bear fruit he prunes
so that it will be even more fruitful"*
(John 15:1-2).

*"If we judged ourselves, we would not
come under judgment"*
(1 Corinthians 11:31).

Response:

Make a list of the things you are trying to control and what is controlling you. Then determine to submit everything to the Lordship of Jesus.

9

Lord, I Want to Be a Christian in My Heart

I commit to being steadfast...

s a new Christian, it was with great enthusiasm that I announced to my pastor, Dr. E.V. Hill, "I want to grow up quickly into a mature believer."

Dr. Hill smiled and replied, "Bunny, you can't ripen a peach with a blow torch. It develops when the sun shines on it day after day."

I've long since learned that my pastor was so right. Christian believers are like God's peaches. As the Son shines on us every day, we continue to develop into people who are pleasing to Him. There's no such thing as instant maturity. Faith doesn't grow up overnight. We have to be resolute in our pursuit of spiritual excellence. That's why *steadfastness* is the seventh Secret every woman wants to know.

> *"...as a Christian you can do anything you desire. The only requirement is that you first 'love the Lord with all your heart, all your soul, and all your strength, and then love your neighbor as yourself.' After that, you can do anything you want."*

Since giving my heart to the Lord in 1973, I have noticed a tremendous increase in the number of Christian conferences, seminars, books, and tapes. We've got all kinds of "blowtorches," available to turn us into Super Christians overnight. We can learn from innumerable sources and experts what to do and what not to do, what to say and what not to say, what to think and what not to think. Yet in spite of all this, far too many people are pursuing their own selfish agendas and prideful plans and calling it Christianity.

Someone once said to the late evangelist Tom Skinner, "It seems like I *can't* do anything as a Christian. All I hear is don't do this and don't do that."

Rev. Skinner answered, "On the contrary, as a Christian you can do anything you desire. The only requirement is that you first 'love the Lord with *all* your heart, *all* your soul, and *all* your strength, and then love your neighbor as yourself.' After that, you can do anything you want."

To quote exactly, Jesus lays out His priorities for us in Mark 12:30-31: "And thou shalt love the Lord thy God with all thy heart, and with all thy soul, and with all thy mind, and with all thy strength: this is the first commandment. And the second is this, Thou shalt love thy neighbour as thyself. There is none other commandment greater than these" (KJV).

If there were no Bibles available and these first commandments were the only Scripture we knew, it would take the rest of our lives to flesh them out. Every scriptural principle and precept hangs on those two verses. Yet in our search for more interesting and complicated information, sometimes the simplest of spiritual standards remains unapplied.

Does that mean we shouldn't study the Bible thoroughly? No! Second Timothy 2:15 teaches, "Study to shew thyself approved unto God, a workman that needeth not to be ashamed, rightly dividing the word of truth" (KJV).

But there's more. We also need to "be ye doers of the word, and not hearers only..." (James 1:22 KJV).

"Lord, I Want to Be a Christian in My Heart" is a familiar gospel song from days gone by. Like that song, when the Bible talks about our "heart," it is referring to the decision-making center of our life, the place where we make our choices. For me to "be a Christian in my heart" means far more than my ability to quote Scripture or expound religious ideas. It means choosing a way of life that honors the teaching of Jesus. It means patiently pursuing the right thoughts and actions. It means being steadfast in my faith.

Meditating Upon God's Word

"But, Bunny," you may be asking, "how does meditation work? Do I have to join a yoga class or repeat a mantra or stare at a crystal?" No, please don't do that.

In Psalm 1:2, the psalmist says that he delights in God's Word and that he meditates upon it day and night. To be a Christian in my heart, not only is it necessary for me to *know* the Word of God, I must also *meditate* upon it.

"But, Bunny," you may be asking, "how does meditation work? Do I have to join a yoga class or repeat a mantra or stare at a crystal?" No, please don't do that. That's not what the Bible means by meditation. The Hebrew term "to meditate" describes something like the process of a cow chewing its cud. We literally chew on the Word of God over and over again.

As we prayerfully read the Bible every day, one particular Scripture usually jumps off the page at us. We can relate to it. It usually applies to something we have either gone through or are currently facing. The exciting thing about Scripture is that it is a Living Word, and it comes to us in many layers. Even when it seems to be self-explanatory, there is always a deeper meaning. After all, God inspired it, and we should want to understand it in its fullness. That's why meditation is so significant.

Take for example the story of Potiphar and Joseph, found in Genesis 39:1-20. To sum up the account, Joseph's father had favored him. Joseph's brothers had sold him into slavery because of their jealousy toward him. This young man was taken to Egypt, where he was bought by an Egyptian military leader named Potiphar.

> *Now Joseph had been taken down to Egypt.*
> *Potiphar, an Egyptian who was one of Pharaoh's*
> *officials, the captain of the guard, bought him*
> *from the Ishmaelites who had taken him there.*
>
> *The LORD was with Joseph and he prospered,*
> *and he lived in the house of his Egyptian master.*
> *When his master saw that the LORD was with him*
> *and that the LORD gave him success in everything*
> *he did, Joseph found favor in his eyes and became*
> *his attendant.*

...Now Joseph was well-built and handsome,
and after a while his master's wife took notice of
Joseph and said, "Come to bed with me!"
　　...And though she spoke to Joseph day after day,
he refused to go to bed with her or even be with her.
　　One day he went into the house to attend to his
duties, and none of the household servants was
inside. She caught him by his cloak and said,
"Come to bed with me!" But he left his cloak in
her hand and ran out of the house.
　　...She kept his cloak beside her until his master
came home. Then she told him this story....

To make a long story short, Potiphar's wife lied to her husband and told him that Joseph had tried to rape her. Potiphar became incensed and threw Joseph into prison.

The first time I read that story, I pondered over it. Over the next several months I meditated on its various implications. It wasn't strange that Potiphar's wife lusted for Joseph and was so aggressive. After all, they were in Egypt, which was a heathen nation. But something about the story stayed with me, and I continued to think about it. Then one day I remembered the first verse, and as I meditated on it God took me to another level.

What makes this story so profound is Potiphar's line of work. Did you notice it the first time you read the story? I missed it a number of times. It says, "Now Joseph had been taken down to Egypt. Potiphar, an Egyptian who was one of Pharaoh's officials, the captain of the guard, bought him from the Ishmaelites...."

Potiphar was Pharaoh's *bodyguard.* But he was more than that. He was *captain* of the guard. Have you ever watched bodyguards as they surround the President of the United States when he is addressing an audience or walking through a crowd? Are they looking at the President? No. They are constantly searching the faces and surroundings in an attempt to uncover anything life-threatening or dangerous to the President. Bodyguards are trained to notice people's eyes, their body language, and their slightest movements.

So here was Potiphar, a bodyguard who trained bodyguards to watch for the smallest of irregularities in Pharaoh's court. Was there a disgruntled soldier who had been complaining, who might band together with others to overthrow the king? Which of the court's husbands or wives were being unfaithful to their spouses? That could pose a threat as loyalties became divided. Potiphar was trained to hear the slightest whisper. So as I meditated on verse 1, I asked myself, "How could a man so highly trained to notice the smallest of details, live in a house where his wife was totally consumed with lust for his appointed aid?" I concluded that when he went home he *dropped his guard!*

What Potiphar so freely gave to the world through his profession, he neglected to bring home. In doing so, he lost the blessing of Joseph's presence in his home, noticeably, the increases to his business, and he never knew why. So many of us are guilty of contributing our gifts and talents so freely in our workplace, but we neglect to bring them home to our families.

That insight is just one example of the way the Lord can take us deeper into His truth as we meditate on His Word. I have learned to treasure my times of reflection on Scripture and to seek opportunities for meditation.

"One less thing to do and my mind is still on You!"

Before I learned to operate according to my seasons, I never had the time or desire to work in my garden. But it has now become a daily pleasure as I not only rejoice in God's beauty, but also delight in being a good caretaker of the Lord's blessings. Every weed I pull, every flower I prune, not only adds to our home's beauty, it also gives me a wonderful opportunity to meditate on God's Word.

During my study time in the morning, I write down a Scripture that has a special meaning to me. Later on, I take that card into the garden and it's not long until I've memorized it. As I repeat it over and over again, the Lord begins to open it up with examples and illustrations. I also value time spent working around the house or riding in my car as an excellent opportunity to "chew on" God's Word.

God's Pop Quizzes

Scripture informs us the Holy Spirit is our teacher (Luke 12:12). So when we learn about a new principle, we should expect Him to give us a "pop quiz," providing us with an opportunity to practice what we have learned. God holds us accountable for what He's taught us. If we flunk the quiz, doesn't it seem only natural for Him to keep repeating it until we pass? Of course it does. But sometimes we seem to keep going around the same mountain of mistakes simply because we haven't taken our lessons to heart.

I remember at one time praying, "God, give me a new mountain! I'm tired of this old one. I know every rock, tree, and flower." Thank God, He does answer prayer. He did give me a new mountian. There is something invigorating about a new mountain, a new challenge. But He wants us to get His truth on the *inside* of us before He moves us beyond our present *outside* circumstances.

As a parent, seeing my child responding the first time to a request is sheer ecstasy because I have spent most of my parenting life repeating myself. God has plenty of children, and He has made His counsel abundantly clear in Scripture. It bears repeating that His Word says, "To obey is better than sacrifice" (1 Samuel 15:22). More than all the time, talents, and financial offerings we sacrifice, our quick response to do things His way is what pleases Him most.

Steadfastly Focused

Meditation and focus are two demanding disciplines that can lead us into steadfastly loving the Lord with all our hearts. "God will keep in perfect peace him whose mind is steadfast" (Isaiah 26:3). But how can we keep our minds steadfast and stayed on Him? By focusing on His Word.

I know quite a bit about focus. Three of my children were born using natural birthing techniques. Frank and I went to 10 classes during each pregnancy to prepare ourselves. We were taught how to properly breathe and relax. Next to the breathing technique, the greatest emphasis was on focus. The instructions were to bring something to the birthing room that I could stare at when the contractions began. It could be something as simple as a dot on the wall. When a contraction came, I was supposed to keep my eyes fixed on the focal point, no matter how intense the pain became. When I took my focus off the focal point, my pain would be multiplied.

This same principle is true in our walk with the Lord. Remember how Peter began to sink while walking on water because he took his eyes off Jesus? We also begin to lose our footing when our focus shifts. You may be thinking, "But, Bunny, I work with people all day. I don't have the luxury of walking around with a stack of 3 x 5 cards meditating on Scripture."

Many of my days are very full also. Telephone calls, appointments, administrative duties, and housework keep me occupied. But Christian meditation doesn't require us to go into a sequestered chapel and close the door. It takes place underneath the skin, in the private place of the heart. Almost every day is a busy day for me, but I fit meditation into my life every chance I get. And as I accomplish each task, I announce to the Lord, "One less thing to do and my mind is still on You!"

As we turn our hearts upward, things around us take on a new light. One of the greatest differences between a child and adult is in the ability to focus. Gabrielle's piano teacher tells me my daughter is doing very well, but she has a problem concentrating. How many parent/teacher conferences have you attended where you've been told that your child is too easily distracted? Focus is not natural; it is developed. It comes with maturity. In order to improve our focus on God, we may need to reduce our schedule by finding the courage to say "no" to some of the many demands that are placed upon us.

During childbirth, the focal point helped me to get through the contractions with less pain. But childbirth still hurt! As a woman once said, "It's like pushing a piano through a door." But with my last child, God taught me something new. He took me beyond the focal point and into His very presence. When Gabrielle was born, I experienced childbirth with almost no pain. I'll explain the "almost" in a moment.

I was very upset when I discovered that I was pregnant again. My youngest child was entering junior high school, and at long last I could see the light at the end of the tunnel.

My time of raising young children was almost over, and I was excited about the additional freedom I was beginning to experience. Then came the shocking news! When I knew for sure, I went to Frank and asked him to pray for me because it was something I did not want. Throughout my pregnancy, I never remember being excited. Nonetheless, it was clear that God had made a decision and I would accept it.

While standing in a supermarket line one day, I glanced at the front cover of a popular magazine and saw a picture of a woman giving birth. Inside were detailed photos from the beginning of the birthing process to the end. As I flipped through the periodical, an intense fear swept over me. I almost felt as if I were going to faint. In that moment, I remembered the horrific pain I had experienced during my previous three deliveries. Yes, the focal point helped me to not be utterly consumed and "lose it," but there was no denying the pain. Right then and there, I realized that there was another reason I was resistant to having another baby— I simply didn't want to suffer at that level ever again.

As I slipped the magazine back on the rack, I prayed silently, "Lord, I'm trusting You to show me how I can have a pain-free delivery."

Just like Mary, the mother of Jesus, who did not tell anyone of her pregnancy, I too made a commitment to keep my prayer request to myself. I didn't want anyone shaking my faith about what I somehow knew was possible. I had never heard of anyone having a painless childbirth, except under hypnosis, so there was nothing in the natural realm to help me believe that this unusual prayer would be answered. I didn't know how God was going to answer me, but I knew He would.

In my fourth month of pregnancy, Frank and I were conducting a marriage seminar in San Diego. After class, one of the attendees approached me and asked, "Have you heard about painless childbirth?"

I was stunned. "No, but I'm very interested," I replied.

She promised to bring a cassette tape to our next session. I could hardly wait to listen to it. The tape really did provide the testimony of one woman's painless childbirth. However, I was troubled by some of her other teaching.

"Pray So I Can Hear You!"

One thing in this lady's testimony, however, was very helpful. She said, "Put your arm straight out. Now squeeze your fist as hard as you can. Can you feel the muscles in your arm contract? Does it hurt? (The answer is no.) Well, that is what takes place when the muscles in your stomach contract for the purpose of expelling the baby."

A light went off in my head. What she said was true. But then why was there so much pain in childbirth? As I pondered that question, I remembered my obstetrician telling me that during childbirth, a woman's body releases a painkiller one hundred times more powerful than morphine. So now I knew two important facts: The muscle contractions were not the source of pain, and God had given women an internal painkiller. Something had to be interrupting the flow of that internal medication. What could it be?

Inside of me one word bubbled to the surface of my mind—*fear.*

All at once, I remembered that when I visited the doctor's office as a child, just before the nurse gave me a shot, she would say, "Now, don't tighten your muscles. If you do, it will only hurt more."

That was it! I had assumed that the contraction of my muscles was the source of my pain. But that wasn't the case.

Instead, when I felt a contraction, I would become fearful, tighten up, and cause the flow of God's natural painkiller to be restricted. *That* was the reason for my discomfort. Equipped with my encouraging information, I awaited delivery with high hopes. Yes, Frank and I still attended the natural childbirth classes, but I already knew what I was going to do. I made God a promise that no matter what happened during my childbirth, I would not tighten up with fear or resist my body's efforts.

On November 12, 1991, my contractions began with regularity. The day before they had been sporadic, so there was no doubt in my mind that this would be the day I would give birth. I went about my daily activities and when a contraction started, I would smile and say, "Thank you, Lord, that my contractions are beginning. I can feel my muscles tightening, but there is no pain. I thank you that my body is getting in perfect order to give birth to this child."

> *We will probably not get through this life without experiencing any pain at all. But even in our most difficult times, the discomfort is dramatically decreased when we refuse to fear.*

Then I spoke to each part of my body, instructing it to line up as it needed to.

My muscles and tissues were operating perfectly, and the baby was getting into position. I spoke to my uterus and told it to open. By the time I finished speaking to my body, the contraction was over. And I was amazed that I could not remember the contraction once it stopped. Each contraction was like starting all over again.

I cleaned the house and grilled some chicken in the backyard. At 5:30 P.M., I announced to Frank that it was time to go to the birthing center. He was surprised because there had been no indication during the day that I was in labor.

"Why are we going to the birthing center?" he asked.

"Because it's time to have the baby." Once I told him that, he began making the motions of preparation, but his face clearly displayed his disbelief. And since I had not shared with him that I was believing God for a pain-free delivery, he proceeded to get ready for our regular childbirth experience. He packed up the ice chest with food and drinks, along with the focal point and a balm for my lips. When we arrived at the birthing center, I gave him a magazine and told him I would call him when I needed him.

When the nurse checked me she said, "You are nine centimeters." (Ten centimeters is what you need to reach in order for the baby to be born.) "The baby should be here in 15 minutes!"

It took a little longer than that because they discovered the baby needed to turn in order to get into proper position. Remember when I said I had my baby with *almost* no pain? Here's why the "almost." They laid me on my side so my 8-pound, 5-ounce baby could turn in to birthing position. By that time Frank was in the room, and I gave him his first instructions. "Frank, when I tell you the contraction is beginning, I need you to pray so I can hear you!"

During that 20 minutes I kept saying over and over again, "God is faithful and I will not sin against Him with fear." Even though I remember that time as being intense, I also remember not being overtaken with pain. When Gabrielle Renee Wilson was born, the Spirit of the Lord was present and powerful in that room.

The birthing nurse informed me that it was a good thing I'd had a relaxed childbirth because there were five knots in the umbilical cord and it was wrapped around the baby's neck. If I had tightened up in my labor, Gabrielle's oxygen supply would have been cut off. That same nurse had been hoping 20 years for a baby. She said to me, "I have delivered hundreds of babies, but if I ever have a baby, I want to give birth in the same way you did."

I had a wonderful childbirth experience and discovered a very valuable lesson about steadfastness. We will probably not get through this life without experiencing any pain at all. But even in our most difficult times, the discomfort is dramatically decreased when we refuse to fear. When we keep our eyes on Him, nothing can restrict the flow of God's love and sovereignty in our life.

Needs, Wants, and Desires

In Psalm 23:1-3 we find the familiar words, "The LORD is my shepherd, I shall not be in want. He makes me lie down in green pastures, he leads me beside quiet waters, he restores my soul." One of my daily pronouncements to the Lord is, "I don't need or want anything on this earth. All I need is more of You."

Psalm 23 teaches us not to want, and Philippians 4:19 reminds us, "...my God shall supply all your need according to his riches in glory by Christ Jesus" (KJV). Jesus, our Good Shepherd, takes care of our wants and supplies our needs.

The invaluable inner blessings of contentment, peace, and wisdom come without a price tag; they are priceless.

But we also have desires which, when properly directed, can be fulfilled. James 4:3 says, "You ask and do not receive, because you ask amiss..." (NKJV). It is a written guarantee that when we delight ourselves in the Lord, He will give us the desires of our hearts (Psalm 37:4). But how can our desires become reality? When we allow God to place His desires in our hearts, the same One who generates the desires also fulfills them.

A great deal of anxiety and frustration is created when we become obsessed with what we *want* and *need*. We make demands of God which are stimulated by what we see around us. First John 2:16 says, "For everything in the world—the cravings of sinful man, the lust of his eyes and the boasting of what he has and does—comes not from the Father but from the world" (NIV). This lust causes us to lose focus on Him as we strive to meet our goals of ambition and materialism.

Does that mean there is something wrong with acquiring possessions? On the contrary, when we apply God's Word properly, it is difficult to keep prosperity away. There is a promise in Proverbs 21:21: "He who pursues righteousness and love finds life, prosperity and honor." Prosperity, however, is far more than material. Good things come to us when we calm our spirits and know that He is God.

There is a closet door in my bedroom where I used to hang "wish list" pictures. I believed that if I visualized them every day, I could bring them into my reality. A computer, a luxury car, and diamond rings were just a few of the items I desired. Then one year my room got painted, the pictures came down, and they were never put back up again. By then, I had come to realize that if I got what I wanted by using visualization techniques, God wouldn't get the glory. Besides, some of the things I wanted weren't what He would have chosen for me anyway.

Now I've learned to allow the Lord to give me what *He* desires for me. To my surprise, the material things I've received are much grander than anything I could have imagined. I guess that proves that our Lord "is able to do immeasurably more than all we ask or imagine, according to his power that is at work within us" (Ephesians 3:20). Clearly, God is our Daddy, and He delights in blessing us. It should be noted, again, that much of what He gives to us is found underneath the skin. The invaluable inner blessings of contentment, peace, and wisdom come without a price tag; they are priceless.

"How Firm a Foundation..."

To be steadfast, we need to have something solid under our feet—a godly base, as we learned in chapter 1. A famous popular hymn reminds us that the Word of God is a firm foundation on which we can build our lives: "How firm a foundation, ye saints of the Lord, is laid for your faith in His excellent Word. What more can He say than to you He hath said?"

As we ingest God's Word through study, meditation, and application, it reinforces our spirits. If you are just beginning to study the Bible, I suggest that you begin in Proverbs, which is found in the Old Testament, and the gospel of John, which is in the New Testament. Try to read one chapter of Proverbs and one chapter of John each day, or you can alternate by doing one of each every other day. How much you read isn't as important as your effort to understand and apply the Word to your life. A Christian bookstore can provide you with Bible study guides. A good commentary and Bible dictionary will amplify the meaning of the text and provide you with background on the cultural and historical settings of the

Bible. I also hope you are in a Bible-based church. If not, pray that God will help you to find one.

If you have been studying the Bible for awhile, using a "read through the Bible in one year" guide may be helpful. And I hope you'll generously write in your Bible as you go along. I have been working on keepsake Bibles for my children. My goal is that each child will have her own Bible. Starting from the first page of Genesis to the last page of Revelation, I record not only scriptural principles, but also special things my girls and I have done together. When I go home to heaven, those Bibles will be treasures my daughters can pass down to later generations.

God's Word is the foundation for our lives. And as we learn it, love it, and live it, we are more and more able to obey Paul's instruction to the young church at Corinth. He wrote, "...be ye *steadfast*, unmoveable, always abounding in the work of the Lord, forasmuch as ye know that your labour is not in vain in the Lord" (1 Corinthians 15:58 KJV). If you want to be a Christian in your heart, that's the way it's done.

Chapter Nine Workbook

Reflection:

How much time do you spend meditating on God's Word? How much time are you willing to commit to in the future?

Meditation:

Scripture Memory:
"Study to shew thyself approved unto God, a workman that needeth not to be ashamed, rightly dividing the word of truth"
(2 Timothy 9:15 KJV).

"Be ye doers of the word and not hearers only"
(James 1:22 KJV).

"...be ye stedfast, unmoveable, always abounding in the work of the Lord, forasmuch as ye know that your labour is not in vain in the Lord"
(1 Corinthians 15:58 KJV).

Response:

Select a Scripture verse that has a special meaning to you. Meditate on it for a week and write down your thoughts.

10

The Fine Art of Mentoring

Lord, teach me to be a mentor...

The arena was filled with over 20,000 women, and it was my turn to speak. As I approached the microphone, the bright lights kept me from seeing individual faces, but I was grateful for the opportunity to reach so many listeners at one time.

Two weeks later, I invited four women into my home for the purpose of imparting to them, month by month, the Seven Secrets found in this book.

I've since thought a great deal about those two very different ministry opportunities. I realized that I consistently feel the same degree of satisfaction and to some extent a greater personal fulfillment sharing with the small mentoring group than I did at the arena, even though I was able to address a multitude at the big gathering. Why? Because even though I may only be mentoring four women, I am still speaking to a vast amount of people.

By mentoring these four women in a very deep and meaningful way, I minister not only to them, but to their husband, children and their children's children, not to mention their other family members, friends, neighbors, and members of their church. Countless men, women, and children will eventually benefit from the principles learned by only four women.

> *Who will reach out to younger women and give them the direction they need to become submitted servants?*

Women on a Mission

I've been married since 1973, and much of what I have learned about marriage and life has been taught to me by God. No older woman has ever approached me with the intention of giving me instruction in womanhood. Over the years, I have often found myself pleading with the Lord to show me how to be a good wife and mother. I acquired some help by reading books, but no one came alongside me to help me understand what I read. Even with God's help, it has taken years of trial and error, and many tears, for me to discover the right path. Surely my own journey would have been far less difficult if I'd had an older female mentor to walk that path alongside me.

Titus 2:4 exhorts older women to "teach the young women...to love their husbands, to love their children, to be discreet, chaste, *keepers at home*, good, obedient to their own husbands, that the word of God be not blasphemed" (KJV emphasis added).

That scripture raises several questions. First of all, where are the older women in today's Christian world? What has become of women who are committed to teaching the qualities found in Titus 2:4 up close and personal? Who will reach out to the younger women and give them the direction they need to become submitted servants?

I am addressing the biggest question of all to a spiritually mature woman who has not yet done so: Are you willing to step into a new role as a mentor to younger women in your church and in your community?

Maybe you're wondering why you should be concerned about younger women. Besides the fact that God's Word commands it, there are good practical reasons that you should make yourself available as a mentor. Consider these facts:

- Today's young women, both single and newly married, are faced with a world system that contradicts virtually everything the Bible has to say about submission, marriage, and family.

- The divorce rate among Christians is just as high today—hovering at around 50 percent of marriages—as it is among non-Christians. This is the case even though God's Word specifically teaches against divorce.

- More mothers are locked into the workplace than ever before, and their children are often left on their own after school, getting involved in unsupervised activities and spending time with questionable friends.

- Many young Christian women have never been taught the most basic principles of God's Word or key truths about Christian life and marriage. They have learned, instead, to allow their feelings to guide them, to "look out for number one" and to "do what's best for themselves." This is leading them into both emotional and spiritual shipwreck.

But what qualifies you as an "older woman"? Is it your age? Is it the number of years you have known the Lord? That is a very small part of what "older" means. The definition primarily applies to the degree to which a woman has practiced Titus 2:4 in her own life.

You may have been married 20 years. You may faithfully attend church. You may even know a lot of information about the Bible. But if you are not submitted to your husband and a servant to your family, please don't attempt to mentor. No matter how well you teach the correct principles, the spirit of rebellion, stubbornness, and contention will flow into the younger woman.

How can you know if you're ready to mentor? Ask your husband. He will be an excellent indicator. Or if you are a widow, discuss it with your pastor.

There is a woman in Africa who heads up a major women's ministry. Her conferences draw thousands of women. She is a God-fearing, submitted woman. What fascinates me most about her testimony is that her husband is still unsaved. And yet she has served him to the degree that he encourages her to teach other women. Even an unsaved husband can bless the work of the Lord in his godly wife's life.

God's S.W.A.T. Team

When my book *Liberated Through Submission* had just come out, I was thankful that God had allowed me to write on a very controversial subject in a simple way. But I still had a lot to learn. It would take years for submission to become a natural way of thinking for me, not to mention a desired lifestyle. I could see the power released when the principle was exercised in my own life, but it took a determined and conscious effort for me to continue with its application. With each step of obedience, however, my resolve to walk in this truth became stronger. In the process, I have seen God's message fulfilled and I've discovered that I'm not alone.

Did you know God is raising up a S.W.A.T. team (Submitted Women And Thankful) right now? I know a number of women who are a part of a small but mighty army of older women serving as a specialized force, committed to obey God's Word, no matter what the cost. Does that describe you? You may have thought you were alone. Maybe you've been feeling what the prophet Elijah felt.

In the book of 1 Kings, Elijah was being chased by the wicked Jezebel. He hid in a cave and cried out to God. He felt very much alone and was sure he was the only one in the whole nation who was committed to the Lord. God's reply to him was, "...I have seven thousand just like you who do not bend the knee [to false gods]" (1 Kings 19:18).

Be encouraged! There are other godly women like you who care about living their lives God's way and teaching others to do likewise.

I have traveled internationally, speaking to thousands of women on the principle of submission. And it has been thrilling to see them humble themselves once they understand why God designed submission to liberate, not to imprison, them. Sometimes a woman says to me, "I could have written your book. I've been practicing submission for years, but I didn't know how to explain it so that others could apply it to their lives." The Holy Spirit has revealed this principle to women all around the world.

Yes, God's S.W.A.T. team is alive and well. We are like Gideon's army waiting to take direction from our Savior. We have received specialized training through suffering. We are singularly focused, and we have been strategically placed where we are by God. Even now, God is preparing us for our mission.

> *Thank God we are pilgrims, moving from strength to strength toward an eternal destination where there will be no sickness, no tears, and no death.*

Specialized Training Through Suffering

A member of the S.W.A.T. team takes James 1:2-4 seriously: "Consider it pure joy, my brothers [and sisters], whenever you face trials of many kinds, because you know the testing of your faith develops perseverance. Perseverance must finish its work so that you may be mature and complete, not lacking anything."

We can always be sure that God is hard at work in our lives, but we can never know what a specific day may bring. As we've already seen, sometimes He uses pain to prune us, so we can be more fruitful in His work. In order for us to become mature and complete, we must face many trials, and we must face them with joy. Pain prepares us to be better mentors because pain is part of every human life. Young women need to know how to deal with it in a godly way.

I learned even more about pain in 1996, when an excruciating pain swept through my body. It was more intense than any labor pain I'd ever experienced in childbirth, and it was constant. In the hospital I was diagnosed with Parshnish-Turner Syndrome, a viral infection of my nervous system. To this day, no one knows how this virus enters the body or how it leaves. We only know that it registers as one of the highest-known sources of human pain and that there is no medication to control it. Thank God it only remains in the body for about a week. The illness left me partially paralyzed in my left arm, but in time that problem was healed.

Then in 1998, I noticed that my right arm and hand were shaking. It became impossible for me to hold a microphone while I was addressing an audience. I made an appointment with a neurologist and, after testing me thoroughly, he could find nothing wrong. A short time later, I was sitting next to my father as he handed someone a piece of paper.

"Dad," I asked, "did you know that your right hand shakes?"

"Sure," he answered. "It's been doing that for a long time."

"Does your left hand shake too?"

Dad said no, only the right hand. When I informed my neurologist that my father's condition was the same as mine—right hand shaking, and left hand still—he confirmed that I have a generational tremor. It's in my DNA (although in my mind that stands for "do not accept").

But what fascinated my neurologist most was my left arm. My former doctor, who had been his partner and was now deceased, had recorded the diagnosis in my chart.

The new neurologist said, "I know that if my colleague said that you had Parshnish-Turner Syndrome, then it's true. However, if I hadn't read it in your chart, I never would have known you'd had that problem. Almost no one ever fully recovers from it. Yet there is no sign that you've even been affected by it."

So there we have it. As of the writing of this book, one of my arms is healed and the other in need of a healing. And the greatest testimony I can offer is that it really doesn't matter. I have joy in the midst of this physical challenge. Yes, it is inconvenient and it would be wonderful if the tremor stopped. But until it does, I will endure it with joy.

We all have many trials, and we all deal with them in one way or another. Our troubles are distracting, but we don't allow them to become full-time diversions. Thank God we are pilgrims, moving from strength to strength toward an eternal destination where there will be no sickness, no tears, and no death.

Strategically Placed by God

No matter what our trials may be, no matter what our station in life, we have been placed where we are by God. Our challenge is to hold that ground until the Lord moves us.

One day I was having lunch with a dear friend who was the head of a major women's ministry. She had organized several successful mega-conferences. What impresses me most about this woman is the intensity of her commitment to obey God, moment by moment. The many obstacles she faced while directing that major ministry were always dealt with head-on. It hadn't been an easy task to begin with, but to make matters worse, during that time she had also been confronted with a major physical crisis.

As I sat across the table from her, I could sense that something about her was different, but I couldn't put my finger on it. Toward the end of our time together, she told me that there would be no more conferences. Although they had been a major success, the Lord had clearly told her to stop. She said, "Just as quickly as the vision came, it left."

Interestingly enough, her illness had been healed, and she was in wonderful health. It was clear, however, that she was facing one of the greatest spiritual challenges in her life. God had brought her into a time of rest, and rest was foreign to her. She was accustomed to constant meetings, demands, and decisions. Instead of all the activity she loved, now there was a deafening quiet surrounding her day after day. She felt like a fish out of water, and I could tell she didn't like the feeling at all.

Since I'd known this friend for quite awhile, I was sure that she would rise to the occasion and accept in stride the new place God had appointed for her. He was making her lie down in green pastures because He wanted to restore her soul.

Countless women can teach us how to be busy and seemingly productive, but how many women can instruct us in being still? This woman is being strategically placed for this season of time, and the Lord will use her testimony of simply learning to sit still in the lives of many other women. Being with her helped me to remember that wherever we are, our sovereign God has strategically placed us there.

Lessons in Hospitality

In 1998 I began my first mentoring fellowship. I allowed the Lord to show me four women who had been married five years or less. It was important that each woman had a personal relationship with Christ and a husband who loved both the Lord and his wife. I made that decision because I wanted to mentor these women about being good wives and mothers and not focus my attention on serious marital problems. After our first meeting, I asked each woman to invite a close friend who also wanted to be mentored.

The following year I started with 12 more women whom God had specifically pointed out to me. I also redefined the term "younger woman." A younger woman is someone who has not applied God's principles to her marriage and family. So even though a couple of these participants had been married more than 20 years, they were still young women in terms of their spiritual understanding and application of marriage.

No matter what the age or circumstances of the participants, my mentoring fellowships have three goals. First, I provide role modeling for being a submitted servant. Second, I infuse the younger women with the spirit of hospitality (1 Peter 4:9). And third, I impress upon the younger women the significance of loving their husbands, loving their children, and being keepers of the home.

What qualifies me to mentor these women? Only one thing—my passion to apply God's Word in a practical and teachable way in my life and to share that process with others. One thing is sure—mentoring doesn't appeal to me because of my natural interest in hospitality. Some women have enjoyed providing hospitality all of their lives. Others of us have learned hospitality out of obedience.

> *What qualifies me to mentor these women?*
> *Only one thing—my passion to apply God's Word*
> *in a practical and teachable way in my life*
> *and to share that process with others.*

Let me tell you what I mean. Frank and I were married only a short time when a couple came to visit our home. As we sat talking in the living room, I got tired. So I fell asleep while the guests continued to talk to my husband.

When it came time for them to leave, Frank woke me up and we walked them to the door. After saying our good-byes, they stepped out onto the front porch and I closed the door. I immediately turned out the porch light.

My husband reached over and turned it back on.

"Bunny," Frank said, "when people are standing on the front porch, you don't turn out the light. And when they're talking, you don't fall asleep in your chair." Thank God for a husband who understood the importance of hospitality. I certainly didn't. But I'm continuing to learn, little by little.

Five years ago, I sat down on the stairs in my house and looked across our living room. When we'd first moved into our house 14 years earlier, we had decorated the house, and it was lovely. But as the years passed, my busy schedule consumed me, and my home was not a priority. It was clean, but as things began to wear out, they had not been replaced.

As I stared into the living room, a disturbed feeling troubled me. The area rug had become so stained that we'd removed it. Now our couch sat on the bare, hardwood floor. Feeling more and more uneasy, I looked around and realized that I had allowed my house to become run-down.

I remembered the two couples who had come to visit us a week earlier. As they were leaving, one of the women said, "Bunny, did you notice your couch was torn?"

When I smiled and said, "Yes," I could see the confusion on her face. I'm fairly sure that if I could have read her mind, she would have been thinking, "So why don't you do something about it?"

At that moment, the Lord began speaking to me about the ministry of beauty. When I walk through a garden, visit a museum, or walk into a home that has been tended with thoughtfulness, I feel comforted. The spirit of relaxation seems to dwell in beauty. Unfortunately, there was nothing particularly beautiful or relaxing about my home's interior.

As I assessed the situation, the task seemed too big for me. I didn't know where to begin. Not only were funds limited, I'm not the type of person who likes to shop. I don't even enjoy looking at the kind of magazines that could give me ideas about how to beautify my home.

I spoke aloud to the Lord and said, "Okay, God, here's the deal. If You make it pretty, I'll keep it clean."

Frank and I decided to work on one room at a time, one year at a time. The most important step was simply to begin. I had no color scheme in mind. I only knew that I wanted my living room to be warm and comfortable. I wanted to greet people when they entered and send them the message, "I'm so glad you are here. I've been waiting for you."

I was beginning to grasp what it meant to be a *homemaker*. It would take time to make my home a place of refuge, peace, and beauty. Still, that was my goal. I remember going to the carpet store with Frank to buy a large area rug for our living room. I stared blankly at the vast selection of colors and textures. Sitting down on a large roll of carpet, I put my head in my hand. I was overwhelmed. What if my selection didn't look right? What if I got it home and didn't like it? After about an hour, my eyes fell on a lush, deep-green carpet. Somehow I knew it was the one.

The process had begun.

Today, our downstairs is almost completed and we are beginning to work on the upstairs. As I look around, it is amazing how God has decorated our home. He not only led us to what we liked, but He threw in fabulous deals as well. What delights me most is the one comment I hear most often from our guests: "It feels so peaceful here."

The women from the mentoring fellowships never cease to be amazed when I show them pictures of how the house looked before. They can't fathom the change in our surroundings that took place once I became convicted of the importance of being a "keeper of the home."

You don't have to have a perfect house or be a fabulous cook to have a mentoring fellowship. The greatest qualification is that you have the right spirit. The rest will follow.

Learning from a Mentor's Mentor

I've known the nationally renowned speaker and teacher Devi Titus for many years. But in 1999, Frank and I had our first experience staying in her home, and it revolutionized my life. Devi has been mentoring women for many years. She talks openly about her meager upbringing—not much money but a house full of love.

Even as a young child, she was not satisfied to simply set the table for dinner. Devi had to fold the napkins in new and unusual ways. It was important to her that the table looked pretty. Today she is still a bargain hunter who can take the simplest of materials and make her home look like a palace. She has the gift of beauty, and she has willingly shared it with countless other women.

Walking into Devi's home is a revelation. There are so many things to see. When we were taken to the guest room, I was blessed by its loveliness. The bed was delightfully accessorized with a wide assortment of pillows. Soft lighting seemed to wrap us in its arms. In the middle of the bed was a white wicker tray with a display of fresh fruit, water, juice, a fresh-cut flower in a vase and, of course, Devi's signature intricately folded napkins. I felt like royalty.

Throughout our stay, Devi paid great attention to every detail. As I opened our bedroom door the next morning, I discovered a small table just outside the door holding a tray of hot tea in a beautiful teapot. (I still don't know how she knew when we would be getting up.) She also supplied us with wonderful edibles, which provided a delicious beginning to our day. The tray was accented with fresh-cut flowers and a candle.

My brief visit to Devi's home ignited in me the desire to cultivate the gift of hospitality. I wanted to impart to others what she had invested in me. By the time I left her home, I was refreshed and renewed. Her house of refuge was intentionally designed to minister to each guest's spirit. Devi is a mentor's mentor. By the time I was ready to leave, she had taught me how to fold napkins for my dining room table in unique and different ways, and had also provided tips for decorating on a budget. But most of all, I learned the significance of making every person's visit to my home a special occasion.

Minding the Details

Here's what I hope you're about to say: "Okay, Bunny. I'm convinced. But I don't know what to do first. How do you put a mentoring group together? How does it work?"

Our mentoring fellowships take place the first Monday of every month (except December). They begin promptly at 6:30 P.M. Frank takes Gabrielle to dinner so we have the house to ourselves.

I go to great lengths to prepare my home for these much-anticipated guests. Each woman is greeted with a warm hug, and we begin with appetizers and hot tea. This allows us to have relaxed conversation for about 20 minutes. Then we adjourn to the kitchen, where I start dinner. Unfortunately, these days so many women do not know how to cook, so cooking lessons have become an important element of my mentoring fellowship.

Sometimes we return to the living room for a time of biblical instruction, but if the meal I'm preparing takes special attention, they sit in the kitchen while I cook and teach. My focus is on the Seven Secrets, along with plenty of examples of how I've struggled to apply them to my life.

When dinner is complete, we eat by candlelight in my dining room. The women leave feeling blessed and fulfilled. They also have witnessed the importance of ministering to the five senses God created in us—seeing, smelling, hearing, tasting, and touching. Many of them return to their own homes and—much to their family's delight—fix the same meal the following evening. It's amazing how willing the husbands are to watch the children on the night of the mentoring fellowship. They know that they'll soon be blessed as a result of our time together.

You may have a desire to begin a mentoring fellowship, but maybe your living space is limited. Perhaps your home needs a lot of work, and you don't have the money to fix it up right now. Your heart is willing, but you aren't sure what to do about the details.

The one essential element for a mentoring fellowship is a right spirit. Share with the women you wish to mentor your vision for making improvements in your apartment or home. They'll be able to watch it unfold slowly, from month to month, and they'll share with you the joy and pride of your ongoing project. Just make sure your house is clean and well-organized. It doesn't take much effort to make guests feel warm and welcome in your home.

In my case, I pay for the food that I serve to the mentoring fellowship. It is a part of my ministry budget. That may be very difficult for you, but it doesn't have to be a problem. Women who want to be mentored will be more than happy to join in and bring with them the different ingredients needed to make a meal. Plan your menu and divide it up among the women.

And what about your lesson plan? That's what this book is for! You'll find plenty of material throughout the preceding chapters. You will find valuable ideas in the next chapter, which was written specifically for younger women. You'll gain inspiration from God's Word and from His counsel as He speaks to your heart. But I've learned one thing from experience, and I think you'll learn it, too. Some of the greatest lessons you can possibly offer the young women you mentor will be drawn from your own personal stories, from the way God has worked in you, your life, and your marriage.

> *The one essential element for a mentoring fellowship is a right spirit.*

Chapter Ten Workbook

Reflection:

Are you an older woman as described in this chapter?

Have you mentored younger women? If yes, will you continue? If no, will you begin on the mentoring road?

Meditation:

Scripture Memory:
"Paul said, 'Follow my example, as I follow the example of Christ'"
(1 Corinthians 11:1).

Response:

As an older woman, ask God to show you one or more women that you can mentor. Chapter 11 provides a teaching guideline for each of your sessions.

11
Words for the Younger Woman

Lord, help me to find a mentor...

*I*f you see yourself as a "younger" woman, this chapter is written for you. You may be young and single, starting out on your Christian walk. You may be older in years, but a relatively new Christian. Or you may be newly married—either by years or by commitment. Perhaps you said your marriage vows a long time ago, but since then you have lived in rebellion and stubbornness concerning God's design for your marital relationship. No matter how old you are, that would classify you as a younger woman.

As I finished delivering a message on submission at the Rose Bowl in Pasadena, California, one particular woman in the audience was greatly challenged by my message but did not want to admit it at the time. Christina had been married for more than 25 years to a very successful businessman. They had a horrible marriage, marred by constant bickering and fighting.

When I gave an invitation for women to come forward and repent of their rebellion, Christina sat fixed in her seat.

There was no way she was getting up and coming down the aisle. But once she returned home, she was convicted in her heart. She fell facedown before the Lord, sobbing and confessing her disobedience to Him and to her husband. As she prayed and wept, a great peace flowed over her soul. She has since become a dear friend, and I think her story will bless you.

I Want a Divorce!

When she heard her name called, Christina spun around and glared at her soon-to-be ex-husband. Al was walking toward her down the courthouse steps.

"What do you want?" she shouted, tears streaming down her face.

"Would you go to lunch with me?" Al asked with a small smile.

Christina screamed, "Go to hell!" and stormed away.

The judge had refused to hear their divorce case that morning. And only a few minutes earlier, in the courthouse cafeteria, she'd had a disturbing conversation with her attorney. He had just returned from meeting with Al and his attorney.

As Christina continuously puffed on a cigarette, her attorney said, "Christina, I want you to wait for three months before you go through with this divorce."

"No! I want to get this over with! I want it *now*!"

As patiently as possible, her attorney recounted his conversation with Al. "He really loves you, Christina."

She impatiently tossed her head back and blew a puff of smoke toward the ceiling.

"I'll tell you what I want you to do," her attorney continued. "I want you to think about this. At the end of three months, if you still want to go through with this divorce, I'll find you another attorney. Christina, I don't think you're listening to me. Don't you know that man loves you?"

In the beginning of his relationship with his wife, Al had put God first in every area of his life. But gradually, as he became more and more successful, he started delegating the Lord to the background. As a consequence, everything had begun to fall apart. The Lord finally confronted Al, saying, "You have your priorities out of order!"

A few days after their appearance in divorce court, Al called and asked Christina to go to church with him. For some reason that she herself didn't quite understand, she accepted. "But," she insisted, "just this once."

When her husband picked her up he was carefully groomed, dressed in a three-piece suit. Christina was wearing black sweats and had on no makeup.

During the church service, the pastor asked for the first-time visitors to please stand. Al jumped up and announced, "I want you to meet my wife, Christina." Everyone started to applaud and cheer. Christina hadn't known that Al's entire church had been praying for their reconciliation! One month later, Christina received Jesus into her heart. The divorce proceedings were cancelled.

But for a woman like Christina, making a choice to accept Christ was just the beginning. She had many rebellious and stubborn miles to go. By the time she arrived at the Rose Bowl for the Chosen Women's Conference, she was discouraged and defeated. Fortunately she repented, and not long afterward the Lord allowed our paths to cross. I began to mentor Christina. Even though she is older than I in years, in terms of mentoring, she would still be classified as a *younger woman.*

Let's Get Started

Perhaps you are like Christina. You want to change your way of life. Or maybe you simply want to get your life started on the right foot. Maybe you don't know an older woman who can mentor you. Pray that God places just the right woman in your life, and keep your eyes and heart open to His provision.

In the meantime, I hope you'll reflect on the following 10 steps. Each step will give you specific direction, summarizing what you have learned thus far in the preceding chapters and helping you continue to develop into a godly and virtuous woman. If you're single, apply these lessons to your employer, church, and family. This will help to prepare you for your future marriage.

Step One

> *"And whatever you do, whether in word or deed, do it all in the name of the Lord Jesus, giving thanks to God the Father through him" (Colossians 3:17).*

No matter what else you may learn, determining to do *all things* in Jesus' name and to His glory is the most important lesson of all. Each step we take hinges on this principle, and it should be our lifelong goal and focus. Our submission and service is not simply directed toward our parents, our bosses, our pastors, or our husbands. It is also directed toward Jesus.

Ephesians 5:22 says, "Wives, submit yourselves unto your own husbands, as *unto the Lord*" (KJV, emphasis added). In other words, even though it appears we are submitting to a human being, in actuality it is the Lord Himself who is standing there. We are yielding to God's divine relationship principles. It just so happens that our husband or employer or pastor or parent becomes the recipient of our obedience.

When everything we do is directed at the Lord, it is impossible for us to become disappointed by another person's lack of a positive response, gratitude, or appreciation. *We are not affected because it is not expected.* Having no expectation sets us free to submit and serve because our reward is in the very act of obedience.

Once I began serving God and not man, I found that the people around me were changing in a positive way. I wasn't looking for gratitude, but it has come in abundance. An overpowering peace permeates our lives when the principles of submission and service are exercised in the name of the Lord.

Step Two

"Thou wilt keep him [her] in perfect peace, whose mind is stayed on thee: because he [she] trusteth in thee"
(Isaiah 26:3 KJV).

Because of a medical challenge I was facing, it became necessary for me to have an M.R.I. The procedure required me to be strapped onto a table with a helmet-like mask over my face. I was placed in a tube just wide enough to hold my body in order for medical technicians to record electronic images of my brain. I thought, "No problem. Small spaces don't bother me, so 20 minutes in a confined area will be a cinch."

I started out with my mind wandering, thinking about a variety of things. Then, about 10 minutes into the M.R.I., I began to feel a sense of alarm slowly rising inside me. I no longer wanted to be in that tube. Fortunately, they pulled me out to check something. I asked the technician to please remove my mask, and when he refused I began to panic. Finally he consented, and in that brief moment of time I managed to collect myself. I prayed and asked God to help me.

When I returned to the tube, a song began to play in my spirit. The words were, "There is none like You. No one else can touch my heart like You do. I can search for all eternity, Lord, and find there is none like You." That melody played continuously, and peace flooded over me. I was no longer fearful or panicked to be in that tube. My situation had not changed. I had changed my attitude by redirecting my focus. My mind was "stayed" on God.

Step Three

> "...to this man [woman] will I look, even to him that is poor and of a contrite spirit, and trembleth at my word" (Isaiah 66:2 KJV).

A Christian who is *poor in spirit* recognizes that apart from Jesus we can do nothing. Sure, we can physically make things happen. But in the unseen spiritual realm, we are helpless without the Lord. And that spiritual realm controls our lives. When we understand that only Christ is able to repair and correct any of our life's situations and circumstances, we are, by definition, "poor in spirit." And you remember what Jesus said about being poor in spirit: "Blessed are the poor in spirit, for theirs is the kingdom of heaven" (Matthew 5:3).

A contrite spirit is absolutely essential in developing into an effective S.W.A.T. team member. Contrite means that we are broken over our sins. Self-justification is rampant among Christians today. One of the most common statements I hear among women is, "I know what God's Word says about this situation, *but...*" Too many believers today are resting on their *buts*. Instead, we need to line up with the Lord's instructions, no matter what the cost. He accepts no excuses or alibis.

The last part of the scripture says we "...tremble at his Word." In one sense, I believe that means we are in awe of God. But I also think it applies to those times when we want to do one thing and the Bible says we should do something else. The struggle between our will and His will can actually cause us to tremble, as our flesh wars against our spirit. In the end, with His help, the choice will be made to do what God requires, and our faith will be stronger. As the old song says, "Yield not to temptation, for yielding is sin. Each victory will help us some other to win..."

Step Four

> *"Let nothing be done through strife or vainglory, but...let each esteem other better than themselves" (Philippians 2:3 KJV).*

Wouldn't the world be a different place if every believer practiced Philippians 2:3?

Selfish ambition is a form of idolatry, where we demand our own way, our own success, our own agenda, instead of allowing God to work His will through us. In an earlier chapter, we learned that selfish ambition causes us to do things out of order and out of season at the expense of other people. Vainglory is similar. It means that we want to receive all of the credit and applause for our accomplishments.

People have often commented that I am "down to earth." What they are really saying is that, based on what I do as a public speaker and author, they expect me to show up with a superior and standoffish attitude. But my response to them is, "I'm not confused. I know Who wrote my books, and I understand Who is speaking through me when I address an audience. I fully remember the type of woman I was before surrendering my life to Christ. And believe me, you wouldn't want to either meet her or listen to her!"

The Scripture goes on to say that we should make others more important than ourselves. In 1998, I attended the Christian Booksellers Association (CBA) convention. Ten thousand bookstore owners and personnel attend that convention with the intent of ordering the newest books and materials released. It was also a time for authors to meet and greet the people responsible for making their information available to the public.

I was accompanying Frank, who had just released his book for men entitled *Unmasking the Lone Ranger.* As we stepped off the elevator of our host hotel, a very talented and well-known Christian romance novelist made a beeline to me from across the room. She stopped in front of me and without even saying hello, announced, "I have been waiting a year to ask you a question!"

I briefly pondered what on earth her query might be, and she continued, "Last year I overheard you tell someone that you wouldn't be releasing a book this year because Frank was writing a book. And I just want to know, what does that have to do with anything?"

The confused expression on her face made me smile. I responded, "I wanted to be available to Frank. If he needed me to read his material, I didn't want to be caught up in my own project. I wanted him to have my undivided attention."

I hope she was blessed by my response and that it challenged her to consider her priorities as well.

Step Five

> "To every thing there is a season, and a time to every purpose under the heaven..." (Ecclesiastes 3:1 KJV).

As you can see, since my conversation with the romance writer, I've gone on to write another book of my own. You're holding it in your hands.

One day, during the writing process, my publisher asked to see what I had written thus far. The vice president of editorial made some very favorable comments about what she had read. "But, Bunny," she said, "you forgot a story in the chapter on seasons."

"What story?" I asked.

She went on to recount a personal experience.

At the 1997 CBA convention, executives from the company met with Frank and me to discuss future projects. Frank talked about his idea for *Unmasking the Lone Ranger*, and they were excited.

Someone then turned to me and asked if I had any new book ideas. "Yes," I told them, "there are three possibilities floating around in my head. But I'm not going to be writing for awhile, because it's not my season."

The vice president of editorial told me later that she was stunned. After all, writers *write*. That's what they do. She had never heard an author tell her it was "not my season" for writing. She said, "I never said anything to you about how I was affected by your statement. But I thought about it for a year, and it caused me to question what I was doing with my own schedule. I wondered just how much of it was me and how much of it was God."

Each of us needs to ask ourselves that same question. Out of all the commitments, appointments, committees, and business ventures with which we may be involved, how many of them were God-appointed? I encourage you to spend some quiet time with the Lord and ask Him that question. Be assured that He will respond. As a matter of fact, He's probably been waiting for you to ask.

Fall in love with your current season, fully understanding that it is transitional. You may be faced with difficult challenges, but remember what the Bible continuously repeats: "And it came to pass..." It didn't come to stay! Whatever it is, it can become a blessing if it is confronted with the right attitude.

Step Six

> "He [she] who pursues righteousness and love finds life, prosperity, and honor" (Proverbs 21:21).

Do you remember my friend Christina? Not all that long ago she desperately wanted to divorce Al. Now they are like two lovebirds who want to be together all the time. I have walked with this woman as she has continuously made the right choices (righteousness) concerning her relationship with her husband. Sometimes she cried because it was so difficult. But no matter how much she struggled, she continued to obey God's Word.

I have also watched as she readjusted her financial dealings. She and Al own a very successful business that affords them a great lifestyle with money to spare. But Christina will be the first to admit that, in the past, she has mismanaged money. Whenever things got tough, she went shopping—and it wasn't at the thrift store. She loved buying gifts for friends and gave little thought to the cost.

One day Christina realized through studying the Bible that the money she was spending was not hers but the Lord's. Once she made some right choices about handling His money wisely, God opened incredible, almost unbelievable, doors for their business. Since she chose to pursue righteousness, God has greatly increased their wealth.

What about your finances? Is it time for you to cut up the credit cards, make a budget, and pay more attention to what you're doing with God's money?

Righteousness does not involve finances only. It includes all of our decisions. But when we want to do what is right, it's only a matter of time before God's wealth, prosperity, and honor flows into our lives. Keep in mind those three things do not always relate to money. I'm a living witness that He'll make you rich in wisdom, peace, and contentment.

Step Seven

"Practice hospitality" (Romans 12:13).

Recently a friend and her guest came to my home for a meeting with my husband. I made a light lunch of clam chowder, peach cobbler, and fresh lemonade. After sitting down at the table, my friend pulled me to the side and whispered in my ear, "I forgot whose house I was coming to. We stopped at McDonald's for something to eat and I could kick myself!"

As you've already seen, I've learned a lot since Frank and I were first married. Today, if you come to my house, you can expect to be nourished physically, emotionally, mentally, and spiritually. After all, I never know who I may be entertaining. As the Word says, "Be not forgetful to entertain strangers: for thereby some have entertained angels unawares" (Hebrews 13:2 KJV).

I had to force myself to learn how to cook, but now I love it. It is so wonderful to watch guests walk into our house and catch a whiff of home-cooked food. People breathe deeply, smile, and usually ask, "What is that wonderful smell?"

Take the time to decorate your home in such a way that it looks like you are expecting company. It doesn't have to be expensive. Candles, doilies, potpourri, and cleanliness go a long way to greet a visitor. Stock up on ready-to-eat snacks that will keep well in proper storage and can be pulled out and served at a moment's notice. A selection of hot tea is also lovely, and soft music creates a pleasant mood.

Practice keeping up your home as a single person, too. Before long, you'll always have people visiting you. Besides, it is good training for marriage. Don't wait until you say, "I do," to learn to cook, clean, and fix up your residence. It's also important to develop your intelligence, humor, and physical appearance. Combined together, these are wonderfully attractive attributes.

Step Eight

> *"Train up a child in the way he should go: and when he is old, he will not depart from it"* (Proverbs 22:6 KJV).

As God's people, we are challenged in the Bible to "...reproduce a godly heritage," and that takes time and a plan. If you do have children, there is a tremendous calling on your life. If you don't have children, God may use you to be a significant influence in some child's life who is not your own.

Dr. James Dobson has written a classic book on training up children, *Dare to Discipline,* and its principles are both godly and wise. Many mothers are frustrated with their children, but in most cases the children were never properly disciplined. Instructions have been hit and miss. Some moms work by the "idea-of-the-week" plan instead of consistently applying guidance and correction.

I have discovered that most of the problems I've had with my children were problems with me. When I failed to implement proper instruction and discipline in a particular area, the entire family suffered. But once the decision was made to be consistent, they became better children and I was a happier mother.

Step Nine

> *"Be very careful, then, how you live—not as unwise but as wise, making the most of every opportunity, because the days are evil"* (Ephesians 5:15-16).

How do your spend your time? Do you waste it or invest it? Time is like money, except once it's spent, you can never get it back. That makes time more precious than financial gain.

I hope you are investing your time in your husband and children. When we fail to do this as married women, we are guilty of time-mismanagement. Being a good homemaker and caretaker demands an enormous commitment. And whether you're married or single, remember that just as our money is the Lord's, so is our time.

Have you ever taken a long, hard look at your schedule? It, along with your checkbook, will tell you a lot about your priorities. God has given us an unknown number of minutes, hours, days, weeks, and years on this earth. And someday we will be asked to account for them. I hope I will be able to say that my life was time well spent. What about you?

Step Ten

> "Your attitude should be the same as that of Christ Jesus: Who, being in very nature God, did not consider equality with God something to be grasped, but made himself nothing, taking the very nature of a servant, being made in human likeness. And being found in appearance as a man, he humbled himself and became obedient to death—even death on a cross!" (Philippians 2:5-8).

There are over 200 pages written in this book, and if they were all condensed into one sentence, that sentence would read: *God calls us to be submitted servants.* If Jesus had not submitted Himself to death on the cross, we would not have eternal life. Although He was God, Jesus came to serve us.

The track Jesus first set in place is the track every true believer runs on. It's a very short track because our time on earth is "but a vapor" compared to eternity. To die and not to have walked in the submitted, serving footsteps of the Master is to be robbed of a very precious gift.

How difficult it must have been for Him to be in human flesh and yet still able to observe the darkness of men's hearts. No wonder Jesus wept bitterly before He rode into Jerusalem. He knew that the same people who threw down palm branches in His path would soon cry out, "Crucify Him!" In Jesus' time on earth, despite the many healings and deliverances He performed, very few men and women were able to see the living God in Him. Yet even though Jesus was rejected and despised, He never strayed off the track of submitted servanthood.

I hope and pray that you and I will do as He did, serving with a submitted spirit our families, our homes, our neighborhoods, and our churches. Through us, God's name will then be glorified. Our lives will be blessed on earth. And we will be rich in heaven.

Chapter Eleven Workbook

Reflection:

As a younger woman, are you willing to commit your life to walking in the footsteps of Jesus? Have you chosen to be a submitted servant?

Meditation:

Scripture Memory:

"Your attitude should be the same as that of Christ Jesus: Who, being in very nature God, did not consider equality with God something to be grasped, but made himself nothing, taking the very nature of a servant, being made in human likeness. And being found in appearance as a man, he humbled himself and became obedient to death—even death on a cross!"

(Philippians 2:5-8).

Response:

If you do not have an older woman to mentor you, start the process on your own using the guidelines in this chapter.

12

Entering His Gates

Lord, I make this lifelong pledge to You...

lthough the Seven principles were not intended by God to be secrets, they do flow from the secret place where we meet alone with our heavenly Father. Psalm 91:1 states, "He that dwelleth in the secret place of the most High shall abide under the shadow of the Almighty" (KJV). A well-known pastor has described the results of spending consecrated time with God by saying, "Much private prayer brings much public power."

Unfortunately, for some Christians, the thought of going to a secret place with God is an unpleasant one. My dear friend Pat Ashley was speaking at a conference about meeting God in the secret places. She pointed out how Satan has denigrated the idea of the secret place. Secrets hide in dark places along with violations and hideous actions.

Molested children are told to keep a "secret" and not to tell anyone. Sometimes they are warned that no one will believe them anyway, or that someone they love will be hurt if they tell. Like molestation, adultery is also committed in secret. Rape is committed in secret. Abortion used to be conducted in back alleys, but even today with its availability, a woman usually goes in secret to have it performed. Most sins take place in secret.

The Bible says that sinful people love darkness rather than light because their deeds are evil. And we're all sinful people. No wonder we don't rush to be alone with God, where He searches our hearts and knows our thoughts. But when we are willing to meet Him in His secret place, He gives us the strength necessary to carry out the Seven Secrets. They are divine precepts, and we are powerless in our natural strength to implement them. He must do it through us.

One of my greatest challenges, even to this day, is focused prayer. My quiet time with God is a daily endeavor. My mind runs off in a hundred different directions, and I am constantly fighting to bring it back. At first I thought there was something wrong with me, but I have since discovered that most believers struggle with that same problem.

> *The Seven Secrets...are divine precepts, and we are powerless in our natural strength to implement them. He must do it through us.*

A Journey to the Mountain

Because meeting alone with God is essential in our victory over the devil, our flesh, and the world, I have been trying to increase my spiritual attention span. Just as I exercise my physical body, I also go through a mental exercise so that I am able to meet alone with God. I picture myself on the shore of a riverbank about to get in a boat. On the other side of the river is a high mountain. At the top I can see the glow of heaven where God lives. My goal is to get there, but first I have to leave everything behind that would call me away from His presence.

Along the riverbank where I am standing, a ticking clock with outstretched hands reminds me that I don't have time to take the trip. Next to the clock are my husband, children, and loved ones, who take up a lot of my waking thoughts. I kiss each one and tell them I have to go. Stacks of dollar bills remind me of the different financial obligations and decisions I need to make. Then there are the various ministries with which I'm involved, uncompleted projects, and a host of current distractions.

As I get in the boat, everyone and everything starts calling my name and pleading with me to come back. I turn my back on them and cast my eyes upward to my goal. When the boat gets to the other side, I begin my trek of walking around the mountain. As the scenes and vegetation continue to change, I repeatedly sing a song as I climb. The lyrics say, "On Jordan's stormy banks I stand and cast a wishful eye, to Canaan's fair and happy land where my possessions lie. I am bound for the Promised Land, I am bound for the Promised Land..."

At one point, as I hike higher and higher, I look down at everything I left on the riverbank. It has become so small that it's difficult to make out exactly what remains on the shore. But now, as I look up toward heaven, the brightness beckons me.

I see loved ones who have gone on before me behind its great wall. I scale the wall and head for the throne room of God. As the doors swing open I see millions of angels singing, "Holy, holy, holy, Lord God Almighty." They begin moving to the side as I walk toward God's throne. Finally I break into a clear area and He is there, just like it is described in the book of Revelation.

I run across the glassy sea and scurry between the elders who are casting down their golden crowns before Him. I kneel in front of His throne and the most amazing peace washes over me. I am in the secret place with the Father. Does He just leave me there? No, He reaches down, picks me up, and holds me in His arms. I look into His eyes and there is nothing else to think about but Him. There are no worries, no struggles, no doubts or fears—only God. I speak to Him as I would to a Father, and He hears me. I lose track of earthly time and it's difficult to return to the riverbank. But when I do, I am renewed and ready to deal with whatever faces me there.

You may laugh at my spiritual exercise, thinking that it's silly or unnecessary. I don't know how you clear your mind and heart so that you can meet with God, but whatever it takes, please do it. Otherwise, you'll find yourself saying the same repetitious prayers, kneeling yet never touching the throne of God.

Why is God's secret place important? Because the Seven Secrets are supernatural. They will lift you above any of life's circumstances and challenges. But they are not of this world and cannot be understood with the natural mind. Consecrated prayer is essential to their successful implementation. And a vision of the Promised Land is a wonderful motivator, especially when the challenges seem more numerous than the rewards.

The Vow of a Lifetime

Now that we're almost finished, I wonder what you will do with the information you have acquired in this book. When the last page is read and the cover closed, will it be placed on the shelf so you can start reading another book? Or will you decide to make the new commitment God is nudging you to accept? The Seven Secrets comprise a way of life, a lifestyle that requires a lifetime of practice. God is calling women from all around the world, married, single, younger and older women, to stand in their rightful place in His Kingdom. Will you answer His call? I hope and pray that you will join me and so many others, and that you will make this vow your lifelong pledge:

> *I am a submitted servant who understands the power contained in both submission and service. I recognize that my success comes from the Lord who in "due season will lift me up." I realize that my sacrificial love may cause long-suffering as I stand in faith, believing God for the incredible. And I commit to be steadfast in the study of God's Word.*

Chapter Twelve Workbook

Reflection:

What was the high point of the material you read in this book?

Meditation:

Scripture Memory:

"His master replied, 'Well done, good and faithful servant! You have been faithful with a few things. I will put you in charge of many things'"

(Matthew 25:21, emphasis added).

Response:

Will you join me in my walk as a submitted servant? Then today truly is the first day of the rest of your life. If not before, I'll meet you in eternity.

Other Books by P.B. Wilson and Frank Wilson

KNIGHT IN SHINING ARMOR
by *P.B. Wilson*
A million-and-a-half women will marry for the first time this year. But many others will become mired in a holding pattern waiting for their expectant marriages to take flight. This book breaks the holding pattern, showing women what to do while they wait, how to become complete in Christ as a single, and what to look for in a life partner.

LIBERATED THROUGH SUBMISSION
by *P.B. Wilson*
If you think this book is just for married women, you're in for a surprise. Submission, as it turns out, is for everyone, and destroys anger and rebellion while setting people free to love and give.

MASTER'S DEGREE
by *Frank and P.B. Wilson*
This book explores the spiritual, emotional, and physical aspects of marriage, then shows how God views, supports, and participates in every relationship. Includes special sections for husbands only and for wives only.

UNMASKING THE LONE RANGER
by *Frank Wilson*
From his longtime experience leading a men's fellowship group, Frank Wilson shows brothers in Christ how they can draw close, support each other, and hold one another accountable.